Stages of Islamic Revolution

KALIM SIDDIQUI

STAGES of ISLAMIC
REVOLUTION

The Other Press
Kuala Lumpur
2005

First published 1996 by
The Open Press, London

Fifth reprint 2005

Published by
The Other Press
607 Mutiara Majestic
Jalan Othman
46000 Petaling Jaya
Selangor, Malaysia
www.ibtbooks.com

Cover photo
Dr Kalim Siddiqui
[*Observer*, London]

Cover design by
Habibur Rahman

Printed in Malaysia by
Academe Art and Printing Services
Kuala Lumpur

لَتَرْكَبُنَّ طَبَقًا عَن طَبَقٍ ۝

Ye shall surely travel
from stage to stage
(Al-Qur'an, 84:19)

In memory of my parents,
my first daughter Shama,
and my son Bilal.

Contents

Foreword

The foreword is invariably written last. I am writing it having just read the final page proofs. It is a sobering experience. On every page there are ideas I might have expressed differently or at greater length. But there comes a time when the author is the prisoner of his work. The option of scrapping the whole thing and starting again is always there; but the right thing to do is to let this one go and start on another book.

The first thing I want to say about this book is that it is not about the Islamic Revolution in Iran. It is about the next Islamic Revolution and the one after that. I had been meaning to write this book for some years. It was intended as a follow up to my 1988-89 paper *Processes of error, deviation, correction and convergence in Muslim political thought.* That paper was originally written to explore whether such an approach would be acceptable at this stage. I intended to send it to Imam Khomeini, but he died before the Persian translation was ready. Instead, I sent it to his successor, Ayatullah Sayyid Ali Khamenei. He welcomed it and endorsed my approach and arguments. After reading the final manuscript of this book, I decided to add that paper to it as an appendix.

When I began writing this book, in October 1994, I did not think I would live to finish it. It was more than twenty years since my first heart attack, and twelve years since my first bypass. An angiogram in 1992 had revealed that all but one of the arteries were blocked. By the time I began working on this book, the angina had been unstable and often crippling for about two years. In January 1995 I spent a week in hospital recovering from another bout of angina, but managed to finish the first draft in April and sent it to my usual readers, including Dr Yaqub Zaki and my daughter Shama. In May, after another angiogram, the cardiologist suggested by-pass surgery, even though the risks were very high, and referred me to the surgeons. On June 5, I drove to Harefield Hospital with my wife, Suraiya, to find out whether the surgeons would take the risk. On arrival, I collapsed and suffered a massive heart attack. Two days later the surgeons carried out emergency surgery. My heart was still infacting as they worked on it. In the next two days I suffered six cardiac arrests, and another three weeks later.

I was in the ITU for a total of five weeks, then in isolation for another three weeks. In the following four weeks I revised this 'manuscript' on the computer twice. I resisted the temptation to rewrite parts of it or to extend the length. It was written under pressure of what I thought was a certain sentence of death. Hence it has the flavour of a last testament. No words of mine can express the gratitude my wife, our children, the extended family and I feel for the many nurses, surgeons and doctors at Harefield Hospital who worked so hard to save my life. When I saw the cardiologist afterwards I thanked him. 'Don't thank us,' he said, raising his finger skywards, 'someone up there is looking after you'. Indeed He is, perhaps in response to all those prayers said for me all over the world.

Now I have to think of something else for my next 'last' book. I am reminded of a saying of the Prophet, upon whom be peace, that if you are planting a tree and you see the end of the world coming, don't stop planting the tree. Doctors say the average life of a bypass is ten years. But the number of years remaining is not important. What is important is that all of us should keep on doing what we are doing now. I have not given up the hope of seeing some more Islamic Revolutions and their outcome, new Islamic States on the map, *insha'Allah*.

Kalim Siddiqui

The Muslim Institute for Research and Planning,
Ramadan 1416/February 1996.

Introduction

The history of Islam and Muslims has entered a new phase of rapid change. Everywhere Muslims are engaged in struggles to establish the Islamic State. This short study attempts to identify and bring together the underlying ideas and processes that are at work.[1] It highlights the need for an intellectual revolution within Islam before Muslims can acquire total control over their history and destiny once again. It argues that such a revolution is already underway. In its early phase this intellectual revolution has taken the form of a new political thought and a global consensus among Muslims in all parts of the world. Also taking shape, in the wake of the Islamic Revolution in Iran, is a transforming historical situation. A number of new Islamic Revolutions are in the pipeline. The Islamic Revolution is viewed as a point in time when all forces of total change in a society converge. The power the Islamic Revolution generates, under a *muttaqi* leadership, defeats and dismantles the post colonial nation-State and sets up the Islamic State in its place. Most Muslims in all parts of the world are already part of this movement. But the processes involved in bringing about Islamic Revolutions that lead to the setting up of Islamic States are as yet little understood, though the need for Islamic Revolutions in all Muslim countries is widely expressed in remarkably similar terms.

The history of Islam has clearly reached a stage when Muslims have realised that they are in a position to initiate, direct and control major change in their societies as well as to play a significant role in world politics. It is important that their drive for change in Muslim societies as well as in the world is directed by a profound understanding of the dynamics of change. Western social sciences have developed many sophisticated theories of social, economic and political change. The West has created a vast network of academic

1

and research institutes that follow, record and analyse changes taking place in all parts of the world. Their work offers a continuous assessment of past and present policies and new policy options available to governments, inter-governmental organisations, political parties, industrial and commercial complexes and their leadership. This is one of the major strengths of the West. The fact is that all of us face a new historical situation every day. The states, organisations, cultures, movements, even civilisations that are most successful are those that can manage, direct, guide, influence, anticipate, manipulate and control the forces of change.

Change from one day to the next is usually small. Changes in the historical situation become more pronounced over five, ten, twenty or thirty year periods. Cataclysmatic or sudden changes are rare. When they occur they are usually the result of undetected or little noticed accumulation of pressures over long periods of time. The absence of change, or prolonged resistance to change, may also lead to sudden or 'revolutionary' change. Not all change is necessarily physical or situational. Changes in the knowledge, perception, understanding and evaluation of reality often have the same effect as physical changes. Thus it is that theoretical, analytical, mathematical, technological, or even philosophical advances may change the perception of reality while the physical form and shape of reality remain unaltered. Most propaganda attempts to build mental barriers against ideas, beliefs or information that are deemed to be undesirable. The current propaganda in the West against Islam and 'Islamic fundamentalism' is of this variety. The West knows that the global Islamic movement has a powerful intellectual foundation. But the West wants to block it out. It does not even want to hear what Islam has to say. To this the Muslim mind has intuitively reacted by regarding the West's policies, actions and propaganda as a declaration of global war on Islam. Changes of perception have as great an impact on history and human behaviour as physical change. Apples had been falling to the ground long before Newton noticed the phenomenon. We shall encounter all these forms of change during the course of this study. It can be safely assumed that every generation faces a new historical situation. All systems of beliefs, moral values, knowledge, thought and behaviour must be able to organise, manage and order change over time and internalise man's limitless ability to learn from his experience.

2

The human brain is such a powerful creative machine that it throws up new ideas all the time. Islam is knowledge as well as an epistemology, or a permanent source of ever expanding knowledge in all fields. Islam can develop, order and organise new information and knowledge. Islam also orders and directs change, and internalises new knowledge born of new theories, experiments, experience, and evolving historical situations. This is why Islam insists that Muslims, all Muslims, living at any one time, must bring the prevailing historical situation under their control. Islam demands that the world's physical resources are used to pursue the goals set by Islam for all mankind.

The *Sirah* (life) of the Prophet Muhammad, upon whom be peace, and his *Sunnah* (precept, example), are the basic models that exemplify Islam's method of historical transformation. The Prophet began with a handful of individuals, organised them into small groups, then into larger goal-achieving systems, until the process led to the setting-up of the Islamic State. This clearly required the development of a versatile political process of incredible complexity and effectiveness. This process as a whole may be called the *hikmah* (wisdom), or the method of the Prophet. The spiritual, intellectual and physical qualities inherent in the *hikmah* are an integral part of the *Sirah* and the *Sunnah* of the Prophet. So far scholars of the *Sirah* and the *Sunnah* have concentrated their attention almost exclusively on the meticulous research and recording of all that the Prophet did, said, ordered to be done and approved of. This literature is extensive and puts the Prophet of Islam in a unique position in history. The life of no other person who has ever lived has been so meticulously researched and recorded by his followers, including contemporaries who knew him, and by an unbroken chain of scholars in all parts of the world since his time. But so far scholarship in this area has been so concerned with the accuracy of the record of facts, events, action and the spoken word that analytical and creative literature has been slow to emerge. The historical situation now facing Islam and Muslims demands that scholars should turn their attention to the formulation of the underlying principles and structural forms of the Prophet's *hikmah* or method. This area of the *Sirah* represents the unopened treasure-chest of Islam and its revealed paradigm. The route to this treasure-house of Islam lies through the development of a whole new range of literature that is based on the *Sirah*. There is no harm in the application of the speculative method to the largely descriptive

3

literature on the *Sirah* that now exists. We must realise that Muhammad, the last of all prophets, upon whom be peace, is a giant figure in world history. It is virtually impossible to distort his life and message, as the Orientalists have found to their cost. Besides, the *Sirah* is also protected by the Qur'an and the record of the systematic transformation of the historical situation that the Prophet brought about.

The vast intellectual energy that the Orientalist scholars in the West have spent in an organised attempt to damage the Prophet's reputation has made no headway. In a very real sense the Prophet is defended by Allah *subhanahu wa ta'ala* Himself. The use of speculative methods of research by committed and *muttaqi* Muslim scholars, with ends and purposes clearly defined and known, may prove to be greatly productive in unlocking the vast treasure-house that is the *Sirah* and the *Sunnah* of the Prophet of Islam, upon whom be peace.

What is being suggested here is that abstraction and conceptualisation are essential processes that may now be applied to the vast literature of the *Sirah* and the *Sunnah* that now exists as a storehouse of meticulously researched data. This requires a new type of scholarship that uses data from the *Sirah* and the *Sunnah* to generate theoretical formulations in areas of political, social and economic problems that Muslims, indeed all mankind, face now. We also need to generate new policy options, organisational structures and compatible behaviour patterns. The *Sirah* and the *Sunnah* must now be used to generate new disciplines of problem-solving knowledge in the short term. These can then be revised to keep pace with new and evolving historical situations. People living in distant parts of the world, and experiencing vastly different physical conditions and historical situations, would then be able to generate knowledge from the *Sirah* and the *Sunnah* relevant to problems and situations peculiar to them.

It appears that for long periods of our history change of any kind was feared and discouraged by scholars as well as by ruling dynasties. This explains the almost total ban on *ijtihad* that is still found in the Sunni tradition. In the Shi'i tradition there was at first an equally

4

rigid ban on *ijtihad*. Slowly, under pressure of conditions, fallacies and contradictions that could no longer be defended on theological grounds, the Shi'i doors were prised opened to allow some controlled *ijtihad* by a handful of *mujtahids*. This slow beginning under a new *usuli* school of ulama ultimately led to changes that made the Islamic Revolution in Iran possible.[2] For most of their history, Muslims accepted change so long as it was *ad hoc* and did not directly require change in theology. In modern times we have accepted the total, some would say sacrilegious, transformation of the physical environment of the Hijaz and the Haramain in Makkah and Medina. The Saudi rulers, acting under cover of a spurious *wahabi* theology, have destroyed vast areas of the physical inheritance of Islam. Most changes that we accept today have been imposed by Muslim dynastic rulers or by colonial occupiers for their own sinister purposes. At no stage has change, its nature, direction and extent, been derived or devised from the *Sirah* and the *Sunnah* of the Prophet. Neither did the change ordered by rulers follow any criteria of good and bad, right and wrong, or desirable and undesirable. Change in Muslim societies, States and Empires has been the result of drift or the dynastic and political needs of rulers at any time. For an example of this one only has to compare the changes that occurred in the Uthmaniyyah (Ottoman), Safavid and Mogul Empires when they were historically contemporaneous. In short, change was not generated, controlled or directed by an intellectual movement that was also part of a political system of Islam, or at least part of an Islamic movement. This single factor alone, more than any other, eventually contributed to the collapse of *dar al-Islam* (House of Islam) and its colonisation by foreign powers.

The literature on the *Sirah* and the *Sunnah* offers an abundanc detail of situations, events, dates, places, names, ages, gen battles, wars, campaigns, decision-making, sayings and so on. All this amounts to description of a very high order. But the straightforward description of facts on its own leads to limited understanding, especially if this understanding is essential as a guide to future action and policy. For example, it is known that the Prophet launched no fewer than 63 military campaigns from Medina. Only a handful of these campaigns were purely defensive in nature and the Prophet personally took part in fewer than half of them. On most occasions the Prophet called a group of his companions, the *sahaba*,

5

often no more than 20 in number, and gave them horses and swords, appointed one among them their leader, and told them to go and deal with a recalcitrant tribe or trading caravan that may be a threat to the fledgling Islamic State in Medina. The military campaigns of the Prophet are a rich source of facts and other information about the situation in Medina and its immediate environs. But little or no attempt has been made to draw a conceptual framework in which the military campaigns fit into a consistent whole in the Prophet's method as a statesman, military leader and a *da'ii*. Apart from Dr Muhammad Hamidullah's pioneering work of nearly a generation ago[3], there is very little substantive work on the conduct of State in Islam. It is difficult to find, derived from the *Sirah* and the *Sunnah*, conditions in which the Islamic State may go to war or take war-like action.

Most Muslims today are horrified by the faintest hint that his military campaigns may have played a part in the Prophet's method of *da'wah*, or invitation to Islam. Today *da'wah* is generally understood as a pacifist activity, more or less in line with the carefully cultivated image of Christian missionaries. The major military campaigns of the Prophet, eg, Badr, Uhud and Ahzab, are described in some detail, but their 'political' implications and 'psychological' impact on the early Muslims on the one hand and the enemies of Islam on the other are only briefly dealt with. How these military campaigns consolidated the Muslim society and weakened the tribal loyalties of the Arabs are issues dismissed in a few lines in the *Sirah* literature. Similarly, there is the issue of 'power'. Clearly the Prophet needed power. But, on the face of it, at least in Makkah, he had no power. What was the Prophet's understanding of 'power'? How did he acquire, use, increase, and generate new power? What proportion of the Prophet's power was military power? What role did military campaigns play in generating more power? Did the Prophet share power with others? If so, how? These questions have neither been asked nor answered in the extensive literature on the *Sirah* and the *Sunnah*. The relationship between early and late events in the life of the Prophet can only be established by means of concepts. It is concepts that help us identify facts and to establish links between facts and events occurring at different times.

Concepts also help us to derive lessons, information and new ideas from facts that may otherwise appear to be unrelated. The organisation and growth of knowledge and its codification requires concepts, hypothesis, overarching schemes, theories and grand theories. These are essential tools of research, understanding and communication over vast spans of time. No academic discipline is possible without them. Historians have only recently and reluctantly acknowledged that there would be no history without concepts to identify facts and that a value system is required to organise them into a written narrative. The consistency of the literature on the *Sirah* and the *Sunnah* over hundreds of years is evidence of the firm grip Muslim historians have maintained over their use of concepts and the organising schema. Even the deviation of Muslim history from the path set for it by the Prophet, upon whom be peace, and the emergence of dynastic rule flying the flag of Islam, have failed to dent the veracity of the literature on the *Sirah* and the *Sunnah*. It must also be noted that hundreds of years of hostile intellectual industry by Orientalist scholars, designed primarily to subvert the *Sirah* and the *Sunnah* of the Prophet, has made little headway. If it was possible to damage or dent the reputation of the Prophet, or to distort his record, the Orientalists would have achieved it a long time ago.

But the only thing that has come close to damaging the Prophet and his *Sirah* and *Sunnah* is the Muslim failure on the stage of history.

The world now regards the historical record of Islam as some kind of medieval 'game theory' that is no longer relevant to a complex modern world. As far as they are concerned, Islam may be a good foundation on which to develop a computer game in which the few always win over the many. But, to them, this is not 'practical politics'. This study attempts to offer a framework in which to arrange our understanding of the origins, achievements and failures of the Islamic movements in all part of the world. It may help them to determine their own place on the map of history. To know how far one has come and how far there is still to go is the beginning of all wisdom.

NOTES:

1. The secular world offers many competing 'theories' of history. Islam reveals the origins of man and the broad sweep of history. Islam also offers a historical method; a method of change, evolution, growth, maturity, progress, achievement, decline, fall and regeneration. Islam's processes of historical change were examined by me in a paper written in 1988-89. It is included in this volume as an appendix. Its title, 'Processes of error, deviation, correction and convergence in Muslim political thought' is a summary of its content. It can also be called a tentative outline of a possible 'theory' of history and historical change in Islam. The analysis presented in this book is based on the 'theory' developed in that paper. The appendix to this book is, in a sense, its foundation.

2. For a brief discussion of changes in Shi'i theology, see Hamid Algar, *The Roots of the Islamic Revolution,* London: The Open Press, 1983.

3. Dr Muhammad Hamidullah, *The Muslim Conduct of State,* Lahore: Shaikh Muhammad Ashraf, sixth edition, 1973. (First published from Hyderabad, India, 1941).

Chapter 1

The role of the
intellectual revolution

An intellectual revolution is a process of revision and correction in the understanding of history and the historical forces at work affecting a people or all mankind. In a sense, for Muslims at least, Islam is sanity itself. All our achievements are attributable directly to Islam, and all our failures are attributable to the distance we have digressed from Islam. The historical situation in which Muslims find themselves today makes it clear that we have digressed and deviated from Islam in many important respects. Intellectual revolution is a process that makes a significant contribution towards the correction of past mistakes and sets us on a course leading to total, or near total, corrective action by all the people acting together.

A vital step towards total correction is taken when Muslims living in a defined area and acting together under a *muttaqi* leadership succeed in setting up the Islamic State. The intellectual revolution gives rise to a prolonged struggle which is opposed by those whose interests are served by the preservation of the *status quo*. This struggle leads to partial successes, many failures, the revision and refinement of ideas, new forms of leadership and, ultimately, to the total Islamic Revolution that defeats all opposition and sets up the Islamic State. All Muslims wish to live in the Islamic State because the Islamic State is the natural habitat of the Muslim. This is because the Islamic State, or the *khilafah,* is the final shape given to the Ummah by the great exemplar, the Prophet of Islam, upon whom be peace. This is why the *Sirah* and the *Sunnah* of the Prophet encapsulate history, and form inextricable parts of the totality of man's historical experience. The Prophet has altered and influenced the course of all history, Muslim and non-Muslim. In the contemporary historical situation, and for at least the last five hundred years, it has been clear that

9

Muslims have not reached the heights of excellence that were their right if they had followed the example and the strategy set by the Prophet. It is obvious, and it is widely accepted, that Muslims have to start again. There is no better place to start than the *Sirah* and the *Sunnah* of the Prophet. Muslims have nothing to fear from the application of new methods of study and comprehension of the *Sirah* and the *Sunnah*, provided this is undertaken by Muslim scholars with a firm commitment to the Islamic movement. These scholars, acting within the framework of the Islamic movement that is engaged in a struggle to establish the Islamic State, will inevitably produce new ideas and concepts giving rise to competing theories and alternative policy options. This may also lead to different groups of scholars arriving at different conclusions. To some extent this has already happened in the past. The various schools of thought in Islam are partly based on this epistemological necessity. What leads their followers into sectarian obscurantism is the insistence that their school's formulation and interpretation is uniquely right or valid. All other approaches and conclusions are branded as deviant or *bida'* (innovation). This has the effect of stopping or slowing down the processes of the evolution of knowledge based on historical experience. It amounts to the freezing of knowledge at one particular time in history. The freezing of a position then diverts attention to the defence of what is ultimately indefensible. The spirited defence of these positions over a long period of time creates vested interests that become entrenched over time. The defence of an indefensible position then becomes their first concern. What should have been treated as a marginal issue based on *ijtihad* comes to be promoted and defended as 'true Islam'. Thereafter, creative energies and researches better expended in extending and expanding the open frontiers of knowledge are being used to defend static and stagnant positions. New scholarship has become a prisoner of the old, narrow, obscure and largely repetitive tracts.

The repetition of the old is in itself not a bad thing. Nearly all human behaviour is repetitive. Habits are essentially behaviour patterns that are frequently repeated because they yield pleasure, security or some other feeling sought by individuals or groups of individuals who have something in common. It is repetitive behaviour that is the essence of cultures, traditions, beliefs and religious

10

practices. Most biological systems are almost entirely repetitive. Every morning, noon, evening and night biological systems perform functions that sustain, support, prolong or recreate life. Often what is repetitive is called normal. Similarly, ecological systems are seasonally repetitive. Within a repetitive pattern of seasonal behaviour new plants, flowers and animal life take shape. What is 'new' is often the outcome of learning and creative energy generated and stored by repetitive behaviour over a long period of time. This explains such physical phenomena of nature as the geological structure of the earth and the enormous mineral deposits that exist in it. This has also been the method applied by Allah *(subhanahu wa ta'ala)* in the development of man. A very large number of prophets, peace and blessings be upon them all, were sent down over many millions of years, before the last of all prophets was sent to complete the process of revelation and to implant in history his *Sirah* and *Sunnah* from which man was to seek guidance for all time to come. Clearly the last of all prophets was sent when, in the Creator's judgement, man's creative genius had reached a point beyond which man was able to guide himself using the Qur'an and the *Sirah* and the *Sunnah* of the last of the prophets.

Examples of man's creative genius are everywhere. Even ordinary men of little formal education who have been engaged in menial jobs over long periods of time have often designed tools that have revolutionised their trades. Such men are not engineers or designers by training. Repetitive labour over long periods of time generates in them the 'knowledge' and 'experience' to design tools that highly qualified engineers would not have thought of. On the other end of the scale, men of great learning often spend a whole lifetime reading, writing and teaching (teaching, incidentally, is almost entirely a repetitive activity) without ever producing a single new idea. Even the books they write merely restate or rearrange what is already known. In most disciplines very little that is new is added over long periods of time. Only seldom do scholars of great creative genius emerge who offer their own formulations, explanations, theorems, hypotheses or even grand theories that substantially extend the frontiers of their disciplines[1]. Compare this creativity in all other fields of knowledge and contrast it with the near stagnation that prevails in the scholarship related to the *Sirah* and the *Sunnah* of the Prophet Muhammad, upon whom be peace, who is unarguably the greatest man who has ever lived or would live. This is not to deny that there have been many scholars who have dedicated their lives to the study of the *Sirah* and the *Sunnah*. Their output has also been voluminous, but largely repetitive. Among Muslim scholars of the *Sirah* and the *Sunnah* there are virtually no seminal figures after the early 'compilers' and the *fuqaha* (jurisprudents) who codified the *Sunnah*. These scholars or *imams* are the founders of the five great schools of thought in Islam - Hanafi, Shafa'i, Maliki, Hambali and Ja'fari. Their work has been used by subsequent generations of scholars, their devoted followers, to impose stagnation on a subject that was supposed to be a dynamic and versatile source of knowledge and guidance for mankind for all time to come. Clearly a body of knowledge, for that is what the *Sirah* and the *Sunnah* are, that was to guide all mankind through all stages of history over hundreds, thousands, may be millions of years, could not be frozen in a limited time frame. By its very nature and purpose the paradigm that is the life of the last of all prophets has to yield new insights and solutions to a never-ending series of new situations and problems that man's drive forward has already thrown up and must continue to throw up far into the indefinite future.

If change is endemic in the human condition, as it clearly is, then the knowledge derived from the source of all knowledge must also expand in quality and quantity to cover all situations that human history encounters. The source of all knowledge must also guide, generate and consolidate change. If this does not happen, then change will still occur, but it will be uncontrolled change leading to decline, defeat, dismemberment, chaos and anarchy. All modern Muslim societies are living examples of societies that have undergone mindless, uncontrolled, unguided and imposed change. Political social and economic pressures, developed in the West in the name of progress, have come to dominate Muslim cultures and societies. The primary cause of the decline of Muslim power has been the failure of Muslim scholarship to produce new ideas from its own sources of knowledge. A body of knowledge that is allowed to stagnate and is then defended and glorified for its unchanging 'purity' can only lose control over events and history. The function of all knowledge is to dominate history and to guide man through the opportunities offered by scientific discovery and technological progress. A body of knowledge, however 'pure' and holy in spiritual terms, that fails to guide change and dominate the historical situation will fall into disuse, even disrepute. It is suggested here that this is precisely what has happened to Islam as a whole, and especially to the *Sirah* and the *Sunnah* of the Prophet, upon whom be peace. The reading of the text of the Qur'an in prayer, or recalling events, words, episodes, even achievements of the Prophet, of the Ahl al-Bait (the Prophet's pure and noble family), of the *sahaba,* and of the first four, rightly-guided *(rashidoon)* caliphs may serve the purpose of glorifying the past or, at best, reinforcing the faith of the faithful. But for the *Sirah* and the *Sunnah* of the Prophet to become once again the engine of history at least two things must happen: (a) an intellectual revolution within Islam that restores the Muslim's behavioural proximity with the Prophet, and (b) the emergence of a transforming historical situation that owes its leadership, power, dynamism, and success to its links with the *Sirah* and the *Sunnah* of the Prophet, upon whom be peace.

Intellectual revolutions within an old tradition, and new historical situations, have to be brought about. They do not just happen, neither can they be independent or autonomous phenomena. They are always interdependent and linked to a series of events and developments over long periods of time. Nearly always they emerge from a common phenological pattern deep in history. Great religions and civilisations that have in the past failed to produce intellectual revolutions have also failed to produce transforming historical situations. This failure leads to the terminal decline of the civilisation concerned. New religious traditions or civilisations emerge to supersede those that fail to undergo the transformation required for their survival. Examples of this can be found in all parts of the world and at all stages in history. Archaeologists have found remains of pre-historic civilisations and cultures that thrived in different parts of the world many thousands of years ago. But the most recent and living example of this is the emergence of Europe from its Christian past into a brutal and parasitic 'value-free', post-Christian civilisation. This happened because Christianity failed to produce an intellectual revolution that might have saved it. Instead Europe experienced an intellectual revolution that destroyed Christianity. In European history this intellectual revolution is known as the Renaissance, which began in the late 14th century. Earlier in the 12th century there had been a minor renaissance which put an end to Europe's own Dark Ages and inaugurated the Middle Ages. Europeans consider the second Renaissance as the first break from the medieval period which they regard as disorderly, chaotic and primarily ecclesiastical and superstitious.

The Renaissance opened the doors in Europe, or so modern European historians claim, to the rise of Newtonian physics and to the industrial and the French revolutions. The Renaissance was followed by its two major-offshoots, the Reformation of the Churches in the 16th century and the emergence of Protestantism. These changes in the European psyche led to the consolidation of the movement known as the Enlightenment during the 17th and 18th centuries. The Enlightenment enthroned human reason as the sole fountain of knowledge, with no gauge or measure, thereby displacing Christianity as the dominant source of belief, knowledge and behaviour. From this belief in the supremacy of human reason have emerged great political, economic and social changes. This secular faith - and it is a faith held as strongly as any religion - is the mother and father of Marxism, Darwinism, parliamentary democracy, Freudian psychology, free love, liberalism, Fascism, Nazism, the nation-States, corporate capitalism and everything else that goes to make up the philosophy and civilisation of the West as we know it today. This is not to say that either the Western civilisation as a whole or Christianity are or were monolithic. They have always been fissiparous as is evidenced by their enormous intellectual output. For this reason, European ideas had a freshness about them that made a great impact in all parts of the world. The export of these new philosophies and civilisation to the lands and peoples of Islam is a phenomenon that has to be explained and understood. How is it that the followers of Muhammad, upon whom be peace, came in practice to accept the philosophy and civilisation of secularism and post-Christian modernism? One answer to this question may be that secular ideas and philosophies originating in Europe appeared to contain a modicum of scientific truth that is also compatible with Islam. This, among other factors, would appear to explain the rapid emergence of a large group of 'modernist Muslims' in all parts of the world. The superficially Christian background of secularism may also have deceived many Muslims. It is also the case that the great intellectual energy and political and military power that Islam generated in its earliest manifestation as a

State and civilisation had been greatly weakened by deviation within it before the secular civilisation, originating in Europe, launched itself on the world. Thus the secular civilisation, masquerading as a Christian civilisation, found itself pushing at an open door.

The political and economic power of Europe, generated by secularism, deceived Muslims into thinking they could draw from the intellectual revolution in Europe to put new energy and power into their sagging history and tradition. Many Muslims of this period probably felt that they had no choice. There was no intellectual movement, much less a revolution, in sight within the Islamic tradition. Thus it was that subservience to Europe became a necessity almost at the same time as it became a fact. In the absence of an intellectual revolution that might lead to the political regeneration of Islam, the continuous subservience of the post-colonial Muslim nation-States to the West is wholly understandable and requires no further explanation.

The question that still needs to be addressed is why the Muslim civilisation has yet to produce its own intellectual revolution. Historians of science and philosophy know that these disciplines and their methods reached Europe from Islam. But for Muslim advances in philosophy and the experimental sciences, Europe might still be living in the Dark Ages. In a very real sense the seeds of the intellectual revolution that saved Europe originally germinated in the civilisation and culture of Islam. It may be an irony of history that this intellectual revolution, generated and driven by Muslim energy and intellectual advancement, occurred in Europe at a time when the civilisation of Islam could not itself absorb it, or take full advantage of it. The fact is that, unlike Islam, Christianity was so riddled with inhibition and superstition against the advancement of scientific knowledge and philosophy that it needed the influence of Islam to break it down. By the same token, the advancement of knowledge could only destroy Christianity, as it has done. Europe, equipped with the energy released by an intellectual revolution that was initially Muslim led, has tried to use its new found power to destroy Islam as well. The arrogance of secular logic dictates that the tools of science and philosophy that have destroyed Christianity should also destroy Islam. In their small secular minds, failure to destroy Islam would cast doubt on the validity of their own philosophy and the experimental sciences. This is why Europe, or the Western civilisation, having destroyed Christianity, now insist that Islam, too, must either commit intellectual suicide or be destroyed by force. The West fears that Islam, despite the ravages of the colonial period and the continued political dominance of 'modernist Muslims', may retain the ability, indeed power, to generate its own intellectual revolution and political regeneration.

In a sense, the world of Islam under Western influence now faces dilemmas similar to those faced by Europe under the influence of medieval Christianity. Europe was rescued by the presence of the tolerant and versatile intellectual tradition of the Islamic civilisation in the Mediterranean region. Indeed, the cultural footprints of Islam on European soil had been so deep that medieval Europe was able to use the influence of Islam to lift itself to a higher level of civilisation. For Islam at the tail end of the twentieth century the challenge has a wider dimension.

Once a civilisation, culture or tradition becomes stagnant within and dominated by others from outside, it needs an intellectual revolution to lift it. The new intellectual revolution among Muslims must set out and acknowledge the causes of their stagnation and decline. Most traditions fight shy of this basic requirement. They find themselves opposed by their holy cows and the unchallengeable wisdom of a 'great past'. The past is great only if it can help to recover lost ground and generate new ideas and strategies for the future.

NOTES:

1. For an interesting discussion of how paradigms in empirical sciences change over long periods of time, see Thomas S. Kuhn, *The Structure of Scientific Revolutions,* Chicago: The University of Chicago Press, 1970, second edition.

Chapter 2

The process of globalisation

Islam has a global presence. It claims a universal and eternal role and historic validity. Unlike the Renaissance in Europe, Islam cannot have a quiet intellectual revolution in one corner of the world and then wait for its offshoots to produce historical results over the next five hundred years. Islam must now generate a global revolution capable of overcoming the colonial legacy as well as the scientific and philosophical pretensions of the West. The West has already slipped back into disorder and moral anarchy. This is guaranteed to return Europe and North America, or the North Atlantic community including Russia, to a condition far worse than that which prevailed in this region under medieval Christianity before the Renaissance. The imposed political 'order' and functionally structured 'progress', achieved after terrible wars within Europe and beyond, cannot be the moral foundations of a sustainable world order or civilisation.

It is here that the West is most vulnerable, yet the West still pursues its short- and long-term goals through such wars as those in Afghanistan, Bosnia, Chechenia, Algeria, Egypt and Palestine. Those who ignite and stoke bushfires will ultimately be consumed by a holocaust of their own making. It is no part of Islam's agenda to destroy the West, while it has always been an important part of the West's secular agenda to destroy Islam.

Islam, having once saved Europe by providing the necessary intellectual impetus for the Renaissance, must now engineer a global intellectual revolution of its own. Only an intellectual revolution that is guided and generated by Islam alone can provide the world with the moral foundations necessary to sustain a new world civilisation for mankind. The new world civilisation must deliver and guarantee *adl* (justice) to all the peoples, races, cultures, and traditions whatever their stages of social, political and economic development. The Western civilisation has not only failed to deliver such justice, it is still determined to retain and expand its parasitic and exploitative domination and control over all the people of the world and their resources.

Whether or not Islam can generate a global intellectual revolution depends on one's view of its history and the current historical situation. Evidence since the Islamic Revolution in Iran suggests that the accumulated energy released in Iran has travelled along the many fault lines that criss-cross the world of Islam. The fall-out of the Islamic Revolution has been at its most evident in Afghanistan, Lebanon, Palestine, Algeria and Egypt. It has also revealed the existence of considerable pressures in all parts of the world. As a result of these events the West now acknowledges the existence of a 'global Islamic movement'. This term was first used in the papers written for the Muslim Institute, London, in 1970s and in the *Crescent International* of Toronto from August 1980 onwards[1]. Events taking place in countries as far apart as Malaysia, Morocco, Turkey, Afghanistan, the Sudan, Bangladesh, Nigeria, Egypt, Indonesia and Pakistan are routinely linked by the media as symptoms of the same global 'fundamentalism', meaning the global Islamic movement.

Clearly a global phenomenon does exist and is active. It has reached a critical stage in many areas. The question which then arises is whether or not the global Islamic movement has the intellectual energy necessary to overcome the legacy of colonialism and continued Western domination.

The Islamic Revolution in Iran points in both directions. Its intellectual roots are narrow and direct, traceable to the *usuli* revolution in the Shi'i tradition in the 18th century. The *usuli* revolution at first had little impact outside the Shi'i school of thought where it was limited to the correction of the *akhbari* position with regard to the role of the ulama[2]. But, in the long-term, what began as a limited revolution within the Shi'i tradition has not only opened up the doors of *ijtihad* and produced a new kind of leadership among the Shi'a, it has also forced the Islamic movements in the Sunni world to re-examine their own basic assumptions and methods.

The Islamic Revolution clearly had the intellectual energies to carry it to spectacular victories over the monarchy, the nation-State, the modernist elite in Iran and their powerful Western backers. The Sunni tradition is too extensive to be corrected by similar adjustments among a narrow band of ulama. Besides, Sunni theology, tradition and ulama have always been open to a much greater degree of political manipulation by dynastic and colonial rulers than the Shi'i tradition and ulama had been. This should normally mean that the Sunni re-examination of their assumptions and methods would take longer and might involve a prolonged process of 'competing approaches' vying for supremacy in the broad Sunni tradition. This process is also likely to be infiltrated and manipulated by such regimes as those in Saudi Arabia, Egypt, Pakistan, Malaysia and elsewhere. Already some 'moderate' and 'democratic' Islamic 'parties', such as the Jama'at-e-Islami in Pakistan and the conservative wings of the Ikhwan al-Muslimoon in Arab countries, have taken steps to try to minimise the impact of the Islamic Revolution on the Sunni thought. The Saudi supported groups, and the colonial-style Islamic parties, are not the only ones trying to keep the doors closed. In Iran, too, there are powerful groups of ulama and bureaucrats who insist that Irani missions and cultural centres abroad should limit their *tabligh* (propagation) to the presentation of the Islamic Revolution as an exclusive product of Shi'i theology. These elements in Iran are unaware of the contribution made by rationalism in the methodology of the *usuli* ulama and the extent to which the Shi'i and the classical Sunni positions have already converged[3].

For the moment, this blinkered view of the roots of the Islamic Revolution prevails among too many of the decision-makers in Iran. In a sense, the impact of the rationalist *usuli* thought in the Shi'i tradition itself remains incomplete. Perhaps this is why the theological implications of the political changes that the Islamic Revolution represents are still widely questioned, even feared and opposed, in the Shi'i community outside Iran.

What is needed now is greatly increased intellectual mobility to allow the free circulation of ideas and experiences in all parts of the global Islamic movement. To some extent this is already happening, as is evident from developments in Lebanon, Palestine, Algeria, Egypt, even in Saudi Arabia. The West has helped this process by using Saudi Arabia as a military base to wage war against Iraq to 'liberate' Kuwait. This has uncovered the existence of a powerful Islamic movement in what was regarded the West's 'safe house' in the Middle East. Desert Storm has shortened the life of the Saudi dynasty by decades. The Saudi role in obstructing the free flow of ideas and experiences across artificially created 'theological barriers' has been rendered largely ineffective. In Iran, too, those who insist on flying the Shi'i flag far beyond their borders when it is no longer necessary are becoming less influencial.

In spite of these pockets of obscurantist conservatism, the global Islamic movement is already beginning to function as a vast 'open university of Islam'. The *Sirah* and the *Sunnah* of Muhammad, upon whom be peace, are the soil in which the global Islamic movement is firmly rooted. During the barren years in the political wilderness it was inevitable that some Muslims would try to secure sustenance and political reward by dabbling in nationalism and democracy. The colonial political culture was bound to attract many followers. What is more surprising however is the extent to which the colonial political culture also penetrated 'Islamic' political thought, even of such luminaries as Maulana Mawdoodi and Hasan al-Banna. After the partition of British India in 1947, Mawdoodi felt impelled to take Pakistani nationalism on board his 'Islamic movement', the Jama'at e-Islami. To this day the Jama'at carries the Islamic rhetoric of Mohammed Ali Jinnah, the 'father of the nation', as an essential part of its own slogans for the conversion of post-colonial, essentially British, Pakistan into an 'Islamic State'. Similarly, Hasan al-Banna's Ikhwan Al-Muslimoon felt that they, too, had to incorporate Arab nationalism into their political baggage. It would appear that neither Mawdoodi nor Banna felt confident enough to communicate with the masses above the din of nationalist hysteria that prevailed in the 1940s. If so - and this an issue for research - then it must be assumed that neither Mawdoodi nor Banna had enough courage or confidence in their own formulation of the political thought of Islam. The enormous prestige and popular following of nationalist leaders persuaded Mawdoodi and Banna to accommodate nationalism and western-style democracy in the programmes of their 'Islamic parties'. This is because the political ideas of Mawdoodi and Banna were not rooted in an intellectual revolution within Islam. They were great men of courage and high moral tone, but they were also men who perhaps did not quite understand the historical situation that faced them and the price history extracts from those who try to change its course. Both Mawdoodi and Banna were ahead of their time. We needed men of their stature now, after a transforming historical situation has emerged in the wake of the Islamic Revolution in Iran. It may be that the political climate of the time was not conducive to thinking in global terms. Both men were products of their time and were restricted by the conditions then prevailing in Pakistan and Egypt. Perhaps Sayyid Qutb was the first major thinker who attempted to bring a global dimension to Muslim political thought. He also attempted to cleanse the Ikhwan of Arab nationalism. It was this that cost him his life at the hands of the Nasser regime in 1966.

The execution of Sayyid Qutb and other leaders of Ikhwan in Egypt and the suppression of the movement by Nasser opened the doors for Saudi Arabia to make an attempt to take over and dominate the leadership of the Islamic movement in all parts of the world. The Saudis began by offering 'asylum' to the Ikhwan leadership that survived the Nasser purge. Thus it was that the Ikhwan 'revolutionaries' were turned into comfortable, middle class 'Islamicists' (a term coined by them to describe themselves) living and working in Saudi Arabia. In the late sixties and seventies these Islamicists, now joined by some Jama'at-e Islami luminaries, began to travel the world to buy influence in existing Islamic institutions, organisations and groups and to establish new pro-Saudi institutions in all parts of the world, especially in Europe and North America. Their remit was to promote what Sayyid Qutb had called 'American Islam'. To hide their true agenda they also printed and distributed Sayyid Qutb's short book, *Milestones*, in much the same way as the Saudi regime distributes free copies of the Qur'an to promote itself as an 'Islamic government'[4]. Among the major institutions these Islamicists established with Saudi funds are the Islamic Society of North America (ISNA; formerly the Muslim Students' Association MSA), the North American Islamic Trust (NAIT), the International Institute of Islamic Thought (IIIT) in Washington, the East-West University of Chicago, The Federation of Students' Islamic Societies

(FOSIS) in the UK, the International Federation of Students' Organisations (IFSO), the Islamic Universities in Kuala Lumpur and Islamabad, and numerous other 'universities', *madaris*, and 'research' and publication centres in many parts of the world. They pay the salaries of a large number of imams in mosques throughout the world and also the salaries of an equally large army of Saudi-qualified *da'wah* workers. In Saudi Arabia itself this global work is not controlled, coordinated or financed by a single central bureaucracy. The main centres that undertake this work worldwide are Rabita al-Alam al-Islami based in Makkah, and Dar al-Ifta' and the World Assembly of Muslim Youth (WAMY) based in Riyadh. In addition to these Saudi universities channel vast sums into the pockets of itinerant 'professors' and their 'research' projects and institutes, publishing houses and *darul ulooms*. The private sector in Saudi Arabia is also a rich source of funds for the promotion of 'American Islam' throughout the world . Those Islamic workers who think they bypass the Saudi government by going direct to the rich merchants deceive themselves. Most rich merchants in Saudi Arabia receive large grants from the government in Riyadh for this very purpose. In fact many 'generous' merchants make a handsome profit on taking it with one hand and handing it out with the other. Between the two hands their pockets are lined as well. The use of merchants as a conduit for funds for *da'wah* in the world is an ingenious device of the rulers from the Najd to soften opposition to them in the domestic politics of Saudi Arabia. It is no secret that the people of the holy land of the Hijaz, where Makkah and Medina are located, have an intense dislike of the Najdis. The Hijazis are also far more religious. The Saudi family, being Najdis, disburse enormous sums trying to keep the people of the Hijaz happy. Other than the tribal factors for their dislike, the Hijazis, for good reason, believe that the Najdis are not sincere in their Islamic pretensions. By funding *da'wah* through Hijazi merchants the Najdi rulers achieve a number of goals: (a) they satisfy the Hijazis that they spend generously on Islam; (b) they dilute the Hijazis' own Islam by offering them an opportunity for corruption; (c) they make the Hijazis more dependent, loyal and grateful, or at least less rebellious, and (d) Saudi State funds get distributed in small amounts among a large number of grateful Islamic workers who visit the 'Islamic Kingdom' looking for money. One has to admire the ingenuity and sophistication of the Saudi system, which is designed ultimately to depoliticise Islam. It is an irony of history that the most politicised parts of the Islamic movement, the Jama'at and the Ikhwan, became willing instruments and partners of this Saudi-American conspiracy to create a self-destruct mechanism within Islam.

The full implication of the fact of Islam's being the final and complete message of Allah *subhanahu wa ta'ala,* revealed through the last of all Prophets, needs to be understood. This means, above all, that whatever the degree of deviation of Muslims from Islam may be, Islam must retain within itself the power of reassertion, regeneration and recreation of its institutions, culture, civilisation and, above all, the State. But Allah *subhanahu wa ta'ala* does not work through miracles. His divine vision and destiny for mankind have to be achieved and established through human effort within the framework of historical change. The first step in this direction is the establishment of the Islamic State under a *khalifah/imam.* This is what the Jama'at-Ikhwan duopoly initially set out to achieve. They failed because they allowed themselves to be derailed by Saudi cash, and because they had not taken into account the debilitating effect nationalist and Western democratic influences would have on them. They have nevertheless made a significant contribution, in raising the Muslim desire for the Islamic State to new heights of awareness, as Imam Khomeini acknowledged after the victory of the Islamic Revolution in Iran.

It is ironic, therefore, that the contemporary roots of the global Islamic movement are to be found in the failures of the Ikhwan-Jama'at-Saudi triumvirate and the spectacular victory of the Islamic Revolution in Iran. Simply by setting an example of success where others had failed, the Islamic Revolution in Iran has drawn the global Islamic movement around it. But the Islamic State in Iran does not as yet have the sophistication to create a support structure for the global Islamic movement of the kind that the Saudis created for the opposite purpose of derailing the Islamic movement. This is probably, almost certainly, because the intellectual revolution that is the foundation of the Islamic Revolution in Iran was a partial phenomenon within one school of thought in Islam. In terms of historical experience, the time has come for a grand convergence of the many strains in Muslim political thought. There is no better area of convergence than the *Sirah* and the *Sunnah* of the Prophet. This convergence does not require new theology: what is required is movement and achievement guided by empirical and rational political thought. We must not do what our elders of an earlier era had done. They, because of their deep concern for the accuracy of the record of the *Sirah* and the *Sunnah*, inadvertently turned the *Sirah* and the *Sunnah* into obscure theology. What should have been a living and dynamic science generating new ideas, structures, growth, expansion and experimentation, has itself become detached from the creative processes of historical change. No two words describe and summarise the *Sirah* and the *Sunnah* better than 'movement' and 'achievement'. Yet the *Sirah* and the *Sunnah* as literature and a body of knowledge have become moribund.

What has become moribund through disuse was meant to be the chief engine of movement and achievement throughout history. It is not that there has been no movement, achievement and change. What has happened is that all movement, achievement and change has taken place outside the framework of their guiding light, the *Sirah* and the *Sunnah* of the Prophet, upon whom be peace. This is true of the history and civilisation of Islam and, obviously, the history and civilisation of non-Muslims. The eventual defeat of the House of Islam and all parts of it at the hands of a *kafir* civilisation is a phenomenon that Muslims have yet to explain to themselves to their own satisfaction. To say that we were defeated, occupied and dismembered because we had deviated from Islam, or from the *Sirah* and the *Sunnah* of the Prophet, are simplistic and unsatisfactory statements. It is like a sick man saying he is sick because he is not healthy. Sickness in biological systems can only be treated if its causes are correctly diagnosed. Symptomatic treatment is never satisfactory and seldom leads to a cure. This applies no less to diseased civilisations, cultures, traditions, religious orders and political systems, States and empires. Islam at its inception was a very powerful and dominant system. It remained powerful and dominant for so long that the onset of disease and deviation was not even noticed. If it was noticed by some, it was ignored by most. The process of movement and achievement cannot be restored and restarted without filling this gap in our understanding of the causes of our decline, defeat and dismemberment.

24

The global Islamic movement, acting as the open university of Islam, has to fill this gap in our understanding. In fact the global Islamic movement is itself a product of a long period of trial and error, or failure to kick-start the process of movement and achievement by partial movements based on partial understanding. This experience of failure in the past, and an implicit fear of failure in the future, tends to distort the outlook and method of the global Islamic movement. While it is right to learn from past failures, the outlook, worldview, and method of the global Islamic movement cannot be based on this negative factor alone. A learning process based on recent failures may lead to partial correction of direction and method; it is unlikely to lead to total, positive and sustained change over a historically relevant time scale. In short, while history is helpful it cannot be a complete guide to the future. Islam is not, and cannot be allowed to become, a prisoner of history.

This is why it would be wrong to treat the *Sirah* and the *Sunnah* of the last of all prophets, upon whom be peace, as history; it is a model, a divine paradigm, of method, movement and achievement implanted in history at a crucial time, that is itself timeless. The timeless nature of the *Sirah* and the *Sunnah* places the Prophet of Islam, upon whom be peace, above history. History does not, indeed cannot, validate or invalidate any part of the *Sirah* and the *Sunnah*; however, history can, indeed must, validate or otherwise the leadership, worldview and the method of the Islamic movement at any given time. History does not tolerate incompetent leadership, distorted worldviews and sloppy methodology. The 'Islamic parties' of the colonial period suffered from all these maladies, hence their monumental failures. This is not to say that the Islamic parties and their leaders deliberately compromised or ignored the *Sirah* and the *Sunnah*. The literature produced by these parties is laced with *ayas* (verses) of the Qur'an and examples from the *Sirah* and the *Sunnah* but this was not enough to save them from error. This suggests that historical experience, and the historical situation arising out of this experience, are an essential backdrop for the application of the *Sirah* and the *Sunnah*. This is another way of saying that history cannot be ignored or put aside for future treatment. The global Islamic movement has to explain the intervening period, from the time of the Prophet, upon whom be peace, to the present time.

A basic assumption of the global Islamic movement has to be that all parts of the Ummah and all schools of thought in Islam will, indeed must, converge on the *Sirah* and the *Sunnah*. The *Sirah* and the *Sunnah* are the ultimate unifying ground for all Muslims. What can be, indeed must be put in a 'black box' as a method of by-passing it, is the divisive theology of the various schools of thought in Islam. It has to be recognised that this divisive theology is a peculiar product of history that has led to the decline, defeat and dismemberment of the House of Islam. But just as the divergence and deviation was a process over a long period of time, the convergence of Muslim thought must also require a historical process and time scale. It is possible, indeed desirable, that the divisive 'religious thought' or theology is 'blackboxed' and allowed to trail along at its own pace. At the same time it is possible, indeed imperative, that Muslim political thought should converge quickly. Pressures for such convergence are everywhere. The client regimes now ruling over Muslim nation-States met in Casablanca early in 1995 to co-ordinate a rearguard struggle against 'Islamic fundamentalism' and alleged 'terrorism'. Shortly afterwards, Ministers of Internal Security from North African Muslim countries met in Tunis for a similar purpose. Soon afterwards the Secretary General of the North Atlantic Treaty Organisation (NATO), Willy Claes, described Islam as 'at least as dangerous as communism was'. He added: 'NATO is much more than a military alliance. It has committed itself to defending basic principles of civilization that bind North America and Western Europe'[5]. The wholesale demonisation of Muslims in the United States, France and Germany; the West's collective support for Serbia's war on Islam in Bosnia; the West's diplomatic backing for the Russian invasion of Chechenia; the continued Zionist campaign of murder and pillage in Palestine; the British support for India in Kashmir, are all parts of the global pressures for the convergence of Muslim political thought that now exists. The fact that the West regards the *Sirah* and the *Sunnah* of the Prophet Muhammad, upon whom be peace, as the greatest single remaining obstacle to their total domination over Muslims and Islam was highlighted in the furore over the death sentence passed on the author of *The Satanic Verses*. The West is frightened of Islam not because Islam is any different now than it was at any time in history; the West is frightened because its diplomatic and intelligence services and the media are reporting strong currents of convergence of Muslim political thought and methods of action in all parts of the world.

It is important that we should examine the nature of this convergence of Muslim political thought and action. That a global Islamic movement now exists is a widely recognised empirical reality. It is also clear that the convergence of Muslim political thought and the emergence of a global Islamic movement are two facets of the same reality. One would not be possible without the other. This is a unique development of great significance in the history of Islam. It is something that has not happened before. Or perhaps this is something that has happened only once before, as part of the *Sirah* and the *Sunnah* of the Prophet, upon whom be peace. But the *Sirah* and the *Sunnah* have not been written as 'political thought', though, clearly, political thought and movement are integral parts of the *Sirah* and the *Sunnah*. This illustrates the challenge that faces a new generation of scholars and all those active in the global Islamic movement. The scholars among them must be part of the movement and must develop a new political thought in answer to the contemporary historical situation. They must set out to break the stagnation that has been imposed on the study of the *Sirah* and the *Sunnah*. They must, operating from within the Islamic movement, derive from the *Sirah* and the *Sunnah* the foundations of a contemporarily valid Muslim political thought. Muslim political thought has already converged in an area that is part of the *Sirah* and the *Sunnah*. Scholars working within the Islamic movement must confirm this convergence, identify the exact conceptual foundations of it, and go on to define and develop the new Muslim political thought from within the paradigm that is the *Sirah* and the *Sunnah* of the Prophet. Similarly, the global Islamic movement, which has emerged more from the historical situation than the work of scholars or thinkers, must also be placed within the paradigm that is the *Sirah* and the *Sunnah*.

Once political thought and movement have been placed firmly within the *Sirah* and the *Sunnah* their impact and potential for achievement would be maximised. Thereafter the forward movement of history will re-establish a circular relationship between political thought, movement and achievement. Each new achievement will enrich political thought which will in turn drive the movement forward to greater achievements. In this sense hardships, or temporary reverses, even some defeats, may actually perform the positive feedback functions normally associated with achievements only. But the factor that turns reverses, hardships and defeats into long term assets is adherence to the *Sirah* and the *Sunnah* of the Prophet, upon whom be peace. If this happens, as it ought, then we have established a direct link between our present situation and the ultimate source of all knowledge and wisdom. It was the loss of this crucial link that led to the decline, defeat and dismemberment of the House of Islam. The precise processes of decline have to be researched and written by a new breed of historians whose primary concern will be the planning of the future and not the justification of the past. So far nearly all historians have set out to justify the version of events, including the motives of the chief protagonists, that endorse the position of the school of thought to which they have belonged. They have also set out to falsify the 'history' written by scholars of other schools of thought. Once the historian is placed outside his 'school', and his overriding concern is the 'movement' that seeks to regenerate and recreate the primary institutions of Islam, especially the Islamic State, then the new literature on 'Islamic history' will have a freshness about it that has been missing so far. And once the movement has converged on the *Sirah* and the *Sunnah* of the Prophet, the quality of both scholarship and activism should reach new heights of excellence and achievement. This will amount to a broadly based intellectual revolution in Islam capable of launching Muslim history to a level of achievement unknown to mankind.

The globalisation process is now complete. The days of Islamic movements and parties limited by geography, nationality, ethnicity, culture and so on are over. New ideas based on hard political facts and the setting of goals attainable by defined and tried methods are now setting the agenda of the global Islamic movement.

NOTES:

1. See, for example, *The Draft Prospectus of the Muslim Institute,* Slough: The Open Press, 1974; and Kalim Siddiqui's short books, *Towards a New Destiny,* 1974, *Beyond the Muslim Nation States,* 1975, and *The Islamic Movement: A Systems Approach,* London: The Open Press, 1976. For a selection of journalistic writings on the same themes in *The Crescent International,* Toronto, see the seven volumes of annual anthologies edited by Kalim Siddiqui, *Issues in the Islamic Movement,* London and Toronto: The Open Press, 1981-89.

2. Hamid Algar, *The Roots of the Islamic Revolution,* London: The Open Press, 1983, pp 9-23. See also Kalim Siddiqui's paper, 'Processes of error, deviance, correction and convergence in Muslim political thought', London: The Muslim Institute, 1989. This paper is included in this volume as an appendix.

3. Ibid. pp. 107-131 below.

4. Sayyid Qutb, *Milestones,* numerous editions in many languages, since 1966.

5. *The Guardian,* London, February 3, 1995.

Chapter 3

Muslim political thought

Muslim political thought is by its nature the most volatile part of the new agenda. Political thought, as opposed to political philosophy, is primarily concerned with the understanding of the contemporary historical situation, its background, the underlying processes at work and the policy options that may be available at any given time. It is therefore prone to the 'narrow view of the sky' syndrome similar to the worldview of the frog that lives in a deep well. It is here that the Muslim mind is most exposed to pressures that lead to short-term compromises. Short-term compromises have a habit of becoming soft options. These then become established habits and develop long-term justifications. Once entrenched as a political system's behavioural pattern, these are difficult to change. At critical times in history, political thought may amount to little more than a concern for immediate survival. A flock lost in the wilderness without a leader or direction would normally prefer survival in the wilderness itself to sudden death and destruction. Such a survival strategy can be a conscious decision or unconsciously accepted and followed as the only available alternative. Survival at any price in the short-term at least offers a chance to rethink, regroup, reorganise and wait for new ideas and new leadership to emerge that might rescue them and their future generations. The nation-States in which most Muslims now live are prisons in which they survive while they wait for the emergence of new ideas and new leadership. The architects and masters of these prisons have allowed us a form of self-rule, known as 'independence', under their overall hegemony. This neat arrangement is also known as neo-colonialism. A common feature of this self-rule is that the political thought of such nominally 'independent' countries and their leadership is still supplied by the colonial masters. Political thought is almost always a function of current or recent political experience. The structure of the neo-colonialist nation-States imposes its own political thought on those who operate them.

Let us look at some examples of this. Prisoners of war held together in a camp frequently try to escape. Their 'political thought' may be summarised thus: attempts at escape keep up their own morale; their participation in the war continues in captivity; they pin down enemy resources; and they are able to maintain their ranks, organisation, discipline and leadership. In this case the prisoners belong to an army that is still fighting and they belong to a State at war with their captors. Muslims living in nation-States do not at present have a power outside their prisons fighting for, among other things, their liberation. Prisoners in a POW camp are only temporarily separated from their political entity. They do not face a crisis of identity, history and long-term future. Their political thought is entirely situational over the short-term. Another similarly short-term and situational example would be an army on the march in hostile and unfamiliar terrain. There is a mountain in the way. The leadership decides that the army has to reach the other side of the mountain, but it does not know how. There are no maps. Opinion is divided. There are those who want to march straight up to the top and down on the other side. There is also an opinion that it would be easier to march around the mountain following a caravan route to the right. And there are those who think that going over the top would be too hazardous to contemplate and the caravan route might also be infested with spies or even units of the enemy forces. The safer route would be to the left where thick undergrowth would provide useful camouflage and resting places for tired soldiers. Game in the thick jungle, they argue, would also be a useful source of fresh food. The more adventurous may also suggest tunnelling. All these are 'political' options. None is in itself right or wrong, *halal* or *haram*, Islamic or un- Islamic. The commanding officer may call a council of war before settling for a particular option. He may ask the officers to take soundings in their units before coming to a conclusion. This is called 'political process' but requires time. If the commander thinks there is no time for a 'political process', he may make a choice and impose it. He may take the whole army right across over the top. He may, on the other hand, take a selection of his crack units and lead them himself over the top.

31

He may divide the others into two groups, appoint their commanders, and order them to march to the other side, one group following the right flank and the other taking the left flank. In this example the goal was clear, the army was united, and there was strong leadership, discipline and organisation.

Political thought is situational. Even to recognise a new situation is part of the function of political thought. Unfortunately, Muslim political thought failed to recognise the true nature of the new situation that Muslims faced in the nineteenth and twentieth centuries. The result was that, apart from a few isolated *jihad* movements in India, the Caucuses and North and Central Africa, most Muslim response to Western intrusion was not only inadequate, it was largely based on false assumptions about the nature of 'Christian' Europe and the Western civilisation. At one stage Mohammed Abduh, an Egyptian scholar and follower of Jamal al-Din al-Afghani Asadabadi, wrote to Lloyd George, the British Prime Minister, in supplicatory terms. In 1946 Hasan al-Banna, who founded the Ikhwan Al-Muslimoon in 1928, asked the Western powers for justice for the 'Arab cause'. In the last years of his life, Banna was under great pressure to show loyalty to the 'Arab nation'[1]. In the 1930s Maulana Mawdoodi considered the British government a 'natural' ally of Islam[2]. Such were some of the glaring gaps in the political thought of Muslims on the threshold of the period of 'decolonisation'. The West's grip over Muslim mind was not limited to those whom the Iranian writer Jalal Al-i Ahmad called 'westoxicated'[3]; the West has also made strong inroads in the minds of leading 'Islamic thinkers' whose loss of a direct link with the *Sirah* and the *Sunnah* of the Prophet, upon whom be peace, was all to obvious. Little wonder then that the West treated Muslim leaders of this period with contempt. The West went on to use such 'leaders' to create client Muslim States throughout Africa, the Middle East, India and the Far East while the Soviet Union was encouraged to keep and absorb the Muslim areas of Central Asia and the Caucasus. What we must realise is that the haphazard and tentative nature of the Muslim response to European intrusion encouraged the colonial powers to drive their advantage home. The West was so certain of its ability to manipulate Islam and Muslims to their advantage that throughout the so-called Cold War, the American camp regarded Islam and Muslims as their natural allies against 'godless communism'. Now, after the Islamic Revolution in Iran and the emergence of an assertive global Islamic movement, the same West regards Islam and Muslims as their natural global enemies. What this shows is that, after many hundreds of years, we have at last begun to establish a direct link with the *Sirah* and the *Sunnah* of the Prophet; we are beginning to formulate our political thought of today from the example set by the Prophet over 1400 years ago. We are no longer following the lead of the West and we are beginning to reclaim our lands, peoples, and resources from the West for our own political agenda. This terrifies the West; hence the words 'terrorism' and 'fundamentalism'. What has changed? Perhaps Muslim political thought is once again beginning to define itself and its worldview and method in line with the *Sirah* and *Sunnah* of the Prophet. This was the vital link with the Prophet, upon whom be peace, that was lost from the beginning of Umaiyyad rule. Perhaps this vital, operational link with the *Sirah* and the *Sunnah* is being re-establihsed to a much greater extent than has been the case throughout 'Islamic history'. Muslims are no longer accepting the worldview supplied by the West. This is not yet conclusively proven. This is where the global Islamic movement's role as the 'open university' of Islam is most crucial and critical. Scholars within the movement must keep checking the position of contemporary Muslim political thought vis-a-vis the *Sirah* and the *Sunnah* on a continuous basis. If Muslims have re-established a link with the *Sirah* and the *Sunnah* of the Prophet in formulating their political thought, then this is the single most important step that has been taken to correct the error and deviance that has been a dominant feature of the history of Islam. The total correction of the Muslim position and direction in history will take some considerable time. Intellectual, spiritual and behavioural deviance that goes back hundreds of years is not going to be corrected in a short time.

The problem is that Muslims have to dig themselves out of a deep, deep hole. What is more, this hole represents an impossible historical situation, from which no religion, culture, civilisation or tradition has ever recovered before. The West knows this and therefore regards the Muslim attempt to evade oblivion as unreasonable and irrational. As far as the West is concerned, Muslims should accept their present condition as more or less permanent. The West would allow Saudi-style 'Islamic States' within the framework of a world of nation-States. This should be enough. For the rest, Muslims should accept for Islam the same status that Christians have accepted for Christianity. In this the West has powerful allies among Muslims. These are the regimes installed in the nation-States by the colonial powers, as well as their ruling elites and bourgeoisies, universities, intellectuals, administrators and many 'Islamic parties'. The economies of these client States are also integrated into a global economy dominated by the West. Such Muslim political thought as has been put together by the Jama'at-e Islami and Ikhwan al-Muslimoon, and other low level 'Islamic parties' in other parts of the world, is largely based on the West's own political ideas. If anything, the Jama'at-Ikhwan approach has convinced the West that Islam has no original ideas, that Islam cannot create anything that is essentially different from what already exists, and that the West has nothing to fear[4].

Yet the fact also is that the West is now in the grip of fear, the fear of Islam. This fear of Islam is writ large on all Western responses to Islam, at least since the Islamic Revolution in Iran. The degree to which the West's fear of Islam is justified is an issue that turns on the political agendas of the West and the global Islamic movement. The political ambitions of the West are obvious: the West wants undisputed global hegemony. The West will tolerate limited religious and cultural 'freedom' and its expression within the framework of a world of client nation-States. Any attempt by any non-Western tradition, religious or otherwise, to carve out and dominate its own territorial base is unacceptable to the West. Neither will the West tolerate the free expression of non-Western ideas. The huge academic and publishing industry in the West accepts only those scholars, Muslim or non-Muslim, who treat Islam from a Western standpoint. Thus it is that Muslim scholars who treat Islam from an Islamic standpoint are ignored and marginalised. Such Muslim scholars are not employed in Western universities, have difficulty getting published, and are generally disparaged. Books that Muslims manage to publish with their own resources remain little known in the West. Even libraries in the West seldom stock them. The West uses its cultural dominance and military power, directly or through client regimes, to try to crush or marginalise the Islamic movement.

In all this the West acts in line with its well developed and defined political thought. The West has a long entrenched view of Islam and refuses to hear any evidence to the contrary. The West's view of Islam has little or nothing to do with Islam; the West has put together a view of Islam that is conducive to its own global interests. As far as they are concerned, Islam is just like Christianity. Therefore, Islam, like Christianity, must also accept the supremacy of the post-Renaissance secular civilisation. In particular, Islam must not interfere with the West's political and economic domination of the world. Any attempt by Muslims to challenge the West's agenda must be crushed. This is the West's agenda in Palestine, Bosnia, Chechenia, Kashmir, Egypt, the Sudan and in all parts of the Muslim world.

Muslim political thought, therefore, has to come to terms with power. Clearly the global Islamic movement needs power. It will need to use this power against the West and its agents in all parts of the world. That the West can be defeated has been demonstrated by the *mujahidin* in Afghanistan and by the Hizbullah in Lebanon. The Islamic Revolution in Iran also generated overwhelming and invincible power. This victory was not only against a powerful regime backed by the West; the Islamic Revolution went on to defeat all counter-revolutionary domestic forces, likewise aided by the West, and to fight and win an eight-year war imposed by the West through its client regime in Iraq. The movement in Iran also went on to establish new political, administrative, judicial and military systems. The new Islamic State in Iran is not free from fault. All new structures have faults that have to be identified and remedied over time. But the Islamic State of Iran is functionally far more efficient and truly independent than any other post-colonial State in Asia, Africa and South America. This is the power of Islam at work in modern conditions. Muslim political thought has to define this power and lay down ground rules for its mobilisation and development. The fact that Muslims from many countries flocked to join the *jihad* in Afghanistan and put this experience to good effect in Bosnia and elsewhere is significant. So far this has happened on an *ad hoc* basis. These are early experiments and experiences from which the political thought of the global Islamic movement has a great deal to learn. The Islamic movement represents a wide spectrum - from leafleting in the streets, raising funds, writing and publishing books, magazines and

35

newspapers, holding classes and seminars, doing research, making films and videos, training workers and so on, to military planning, intelligence gathering, and active combat where necessary. Muslim political thought has to encompass all these and many more activities simultaneously in many parts of the world.

One great weakness of the Ikhwan-Jama'at duopoly has been that their political thought consisted largely of stating the broad moral or divine precepts; they did not think it necessary to produce a political thought to fit the micro situation facing Muslims in Pakistan and the Arab world. They assumed that they would reach their goal of setting up Islamic States without having to fight for it; that a partial political thought that contended itself with repeating the moral precepts of Islam in the political field would be sufficient to take them all the way. They perhaps thought this is what the Prophet, upon whom be peace, had done. In fact the Prophet had started with moral precepts of political behaviour and then applied them to produce a range of policies to fit the situation that faced him and the early Muslims. The global Islamic movement must not make the mistake of confusing moral precepts with political thought. In politics even partial action requires the framework of total political thought. In recent times Islamic parties have fallen into the trap of choosing one, two or a selection of examples from the *Sirah* and the *Sunnah* and presenting them as the whole. In this way, the *Sirah,* and the *Sunnah* have become justifications for the partial and often misguided thoughts of leaders and their parties who had reached their conclusions even before consulting the *Sirah* and the *Sunnah*. The global Islamic movement has already gathered considerable momentum in many parts of the world. Its progress and effectiveness depends upon the emergence of an overarching, all embracing, umbrella of Muslim political thought. Many parts of this overarching structure have now been developed. Enough of a new global Muslim political thought is now in place to justify optimism for the future of the global Islamic movement.

NOTES:

1. Richard P. Mitchell, *The Society of Muslim Brothers*, London: Oxford University Press, 1959, pp 47-71.

2. Abul Ala Mawdoodi, *Tanqihat*, Lahore: Islamic Publications, 1970, p 176.

3. Jalal Al-i Ahmad, *Occidentosis: A Plague from the West*, translated by R. Campbell and Hamid Algar, Berkeley: Mizan Press, 1984.

4. See, for example, Olivier Roy, *The Failure of Political Islam*, London: I.B. Tauris & Co, 1994.

Chapter 4

Towards a global consensus

The existence of the global Islamic movement is confirmed by the observation of common patterns in the political behaviour of organised groups of Muslims in all parts the world. This global sharing of thought and behaviour is not noticed by Muslims alone. The Western media that normally insist that Muslims living in different countries of the world have nothing in common and cannot act together, has also observed these patterns. The West claims to be startled by it. They are reporting the emergence of a global Islamic movement and identifying it as a new enemy of the West, branding it as fundamentalist and terrorist. But common patterns in Muslim behaviour in distant lands are not new. Some fifty years ago all Muslim countries had nationalist parties, led by 'fathers of the nation', that demanded independence from Western colonial powers. These parties and their leaders were not accused of belonging to a global Muslim nationalist movement that was bent on destroying or threatening the West and its global interests. This is because the nationalist parties and their leaders were the colonial powers' own creation. They were conscious or unconscious partners in the West's global agenda to turn the colonies into client and subservient nation-States. The West was then engaged in transforming the world of a handful of competing empires into a world composed of a large number of weak and dependent nation-States divided into spheres of influence. What was called 'decolonisation' was in fact a more sinister process of restructuring the colonial system. It is this that later came to be known as neo-colonialism. The fact is that the secular nationalist parties, and the 'Islamic parties' of this period which took nationalism on board, posed no threat to the new system the West was setting up to take its global domination into a new phase of stability and permanence. The United Nations was created as a club of formal colonial powers to control the world through the Security Council.

What has changed is that the West now detects a new mood among Muslims in all parts of the world. This mood has risen above nationalism, geographical frontiers, and racial, cultural and linguistic boundaries. In other words, this mood is global. This mood among Muslims does not stop at disenchantment with the West, Western sponsored leaders and Western economic and cultural oppression and exploitation; this mood has strong anti-nationalist overtones as well. Beyond the recent colonial experience, Muslims have no record of using national loyalties for the purpose of expressing political identities. Nationalism is the Muslim world is a Western creation and imposition. Throughout history Muslims created and successfully ruled over large empires that included many nationalities. They did not resort to using the national identities of their people to set up political systems or to establish or claim political legitimacy. Such ideas as those of racial superiority, 'fighting for King and Country', and 'my country right or wrong' never occurred to Muslim rulers.

Now the moral ethos of the new Muslim leadership at the grassroots level is also changing. Although the Westernised elites are still in charge, except in Iran, their grip is slipping. In every Muslim nation-State this elite stands exposed as corrupt, incompetent and impotent. None of the nation-States has solved the problems of political legitimacy, social cohesion, law and order, justice, equity and economic development. All political systems in post-colonial States are unstable and suffer from a total lack of legitimacy based on popular support, history or law. Virtually all of them, including those with a thin democratic veneer, are military or bureaucratic autocracies.It is this post-colonial disorder, created and exploited by the West, that is threatened by the global Islamic movement.

The global Islamic movement is not calling for the reform of the post-colonial order, for more popular participation in 'democracy', for better and clean administration, or for the redistribution of wealth and economic opportunities; instead, Islam seeks to overturn the system, wrest power from the Westernised elites, dismantle the nation-

States and their support structures, terminate the West's political, economic and cultural domination and replace all this with new Islamic States in all parts of the Muslim world. The new Islamic movement will be content with nothing short of a total Revolution to end the colonial legacy for good. These goals are now deeply ingrained in the political mindset of the Muslim masses in all parts of the world. What is more, this mindset is not exclusive to the deprived classes: a large proportion of the young professional classes and students among the Westernised elites are actively promoting it. The new global Islamic movement includes all social classes among all Muslims living all over the world, including the substantial Muslim minorities in the West.

There is a curious fact of Muslim history that we must now note. Throughout their long political history as empire builders and rulers, at no stage did Muslims develop a political consensus on any significant scale. This is probably because dominant political systems that are not threatened by internal dissent do not need to develop political consensus. The acceptance of the legitimacy of the dominant authority, expressed by the absence of internal dissent, was itself a form of consensus. The fact also is that very early in its history, the caliphate did in fact experience widespread dissent. This dissent led to the murder of the third caliph, Othman, and caused Ali, the fourth caliph, to fight wars to put down rebellion. Ali, too, was assassinated. The Umaiyyads, the first dynastic rulers in the history of Islam, had come to power by successful dissent and rebellion. Despite this fundamental illegitimacy, subsequent dynastic rulers continued to impose and maintain stability and consensus for long periods of time. This gave rise, certainly in the Sunni school of thought, to the doctrine that forbade, subject to certain conditions, rebellion against the ruler of the day[1]. This doctrine eventually helped even the colonial powers to secure endorsement of legitimacy for their rule from many influential Sunni ulama. It would appear from this that political consensus in Muslim history has nearly always been *post facto* acceptance of Muslim dynastic rule, and more recently the acceptance of rule by non-Muslim occupiers of Muslim lands. This doctrine amounted to the rulers' right to obedience under all circumstances. This doctrine is still the bedrock of 'Islamic legitimacy' that is claimed by such rulers as those of Saudi Arabia. The entire political programme of cooperation with the British, promoted by such men as Sir Sayyid Ahmed Khan of India, appears to have been based on this doctrine. Traces of this doctrine are also found in the writings of Mawdoodi and many Arab writers of this period.

A major hallmark of the political thought of the modern global Islamic movement is that this pernicious doctrine has no place in it. The thought of such men as Sayyid Qutb and Imam Khomeini, and the example set by the Islamic Revolution in Iran, have totally superceded such ideas. The fact that the Islamic State in Iran has survived Western sponsored military invasion, counter-revolution, and diplomatic and economic boycott has also eroded the case for dependence on the United States that was advanced by such leading Muslim nation-States as Saudi Arabia, Pakistan, Turkey and Egypt. An uncompromising hostility to pro-Western regimes, and rejection of foreign policies that accept the hegemony of the West, are also hallmarks of the political thought of the global Islamic movement. What is also unique is that these ideas and attitudes are no longer limited to some regions of the world. These ideas and attitudes are shared and universally held as self-evident truths among Muslims in all parts of the world at the same time. It is probably no exaggeration to say that at no other time in history have political ideas and attitudes among Muslims become so universalised in their acceptability and passionate in their expression as now. Two factors about these ideas held commonly by all Muslims across the cultural, racial, national, linguistic spectrum should be noted. The first is that all these ideas are modern and based on the empirical conditions prevailing in the world at this time. At the same time these ideas have strong roots in theology that is common to all schools of thought in Islam; therefore they are above issues of theological or sectarian disputations. These ideas, or this mosaic of new political thought among Muslims, provide a living and dynamic demonstration of the unity of the Ummah. They give a lie to the propaganda that claims that Muslims are too divided to cooperate. The fact is that people who can think together can also act together, especially in the political arena. Indeed, politics are primarily about persuading people to think together. If they think together, and their political ideas have a close resemblance, then they are likely to pursue or support common programmes of action in pursuit of broadly common goals. This situation already exists among Muslims in all parts of the world.

The emergence of political consensus amongst Muslims all over the world is a most exciting development in the history of Islam and Muslims. This is all the more amazing because Muslims are behind, almost backward, in all forms of technology, especially information technology. In the arena of the global print and electronic media, Muslims have no presence. There is not a single Muslim newspaper or magazine with a significant global circulation. Nearly all print and electronic media in the Muslim world is local and largely controlled by the pro-Western secular regimes. The few 'Islamic' newspapers and magazines that exist tend to follow the 'moderate' line of the Jama'at/Ikhwan duopoly. The media in post-revolutionary Iran are poor in quality. Political thought in the Irani media is limited to a few slogans and extensive quotations from Shi'i texts. No Irani newspaper or magazine has achieved significant circulation outside Iran. However, the intellectual output within Iran, almost entirely in Farsi, is massive.

Iran is a very literate society with literacy rate approaching 90 percent. Print orders for new books run into hundreds of thousands. The attention given to the 'cultural revolution' was almost as great as the attention given to political change. The closing down of the universities for three years, the thorough revision of curricula and reading material, and the replacement of teaching staff whose commitment to Islam was doubtful, were truly revolutionary steps ordered by Imam Khomeini. But none of this had any significant effect on Muslims outside Iran.

Practically the only exception to all this is the *Crescent International* of Toronto. This fortnightly 'newsmagazine' was launched from the basement of its founders, Latif Owaisi and his wife Zahida, in 1972. Initially it had a small circulation among mainly Pakistani immigrants around Toronto. In 1975 Zafar Bangash, a young graduate civil engineer from London, also of Pakistani origin, migrated to Canada. He became editor of the *Crescent International*. Although it was a community paper it had strong views on world affairs affecting Muslims. During 1978-79, the *Crescent International* came out strongly in support of the Islamic Revolution. In London a similar position was taken up by the Muslim Institute. Zafar Bangash, during his student days in London, had been a member of the Muslim

Institute's preparatory committee. In 1980 the Muslim Institute helped to relaunch the *Crescent International* as the 'newsmagazine of the Islamic movement'. Since then, this twice-monthly magazine has performed a multiplicity of functions. It was at once a propaganda organ, an academic journal, and a news and feature service for the world's fringe Islamic media. Academics who were inspired by the Islamic Revolution wrote for it, journalists whose own papers would not publish their work found space in it, and small Islamic weeklies and monthlies throughout the world freely lifted and translated its material. This greatly lifted the quality of the fringe Islamic media throughout the world. In the early years after the Islamic Revolution, even the Iranian media were full of material lifted from this small newsmagazine published from Toronto. Material from the *Crescent International* was also edited and compiled in an annual anthology under the title *Issues in the Islamic Movement.*

The emergence of a global political consensus among Muslims the world over at the same time cannot therefore be attributed to the Muslim media. Perhaps the most important factor was that the Islamic Revolution lifted Islam into the world's headlines to a degree that had not happened before in modern times. Until the Islamic Revolution, Islam was mentioned in the media only as a 'religion', and even then the religion of such people as the Saudis and such other Arab and Muslim leaders who were happy to accept subservience as their permanent condition. Islam's role in the Western media was little more than to support the now defunct 'free world' bloc against communism. The Western media had no experience of handling something as big as the Islamic Revolution and its global fallout. The figure of Imam Khomeini was not only photogenic, it also confirmed Western view of Islam as something medieval and out of this world. And no one could have been better dressed up for a medieval role than Imam Khomeini when he burst upon the world scene with his arrival in Paris in October 1978. From then on Imam Khomeini's walks in the French countryside, his prayer meetings and anti-Western public utterances were covered by the world's television networks almost 24 hours a day. At the same time, the Shah of Iran was presented as a modernising ruler being threatened by 'forces of darkness'. The media were also reporting and showing scenes of popular revolt against Pehlavi rule on the streets of Tehran and other Iranian cities.

The Islamic Revolution became the world's first fully televised revolution. The Western media no doubt succeeded in turning Western opinion against Islam, Imam Khomeini and the Islamic Revolution, but Muslim viewers all over the world got a different message. They saw with their own eyes the power of Islam victorious against the 'forces of darkness' of the West. The concerted Western propaganda against the Islamic Revolution and its leadership had the opposite effect on Muslims than the one intended. There was hardly a Muslim in the world who was not thrilled by the victory of the Islamic Revolution and the leadership of Imam Khomeini.

There are certain correcting mechanisms in Islam that only Muslims understand. One such mechanism is the *Sirah* and the *Sunnah* of the Prophet, upon whom be peace. At crucial moments in history the memory of the *Sirah* and the *Sunnah* acts as a filter in the Muslim mind. This filter converts negative inputs into positive ones. The Quraish of Makkah had made the mistake 1400 years ago of trying to denigrate the Prophet. The West now made the same mistake by trying to denigrate the Islamic Revolution and Imam Khomeini. The West's propaganda against the Islamic Revolution helped to lift Muslim political thought to a new level of global consensus and commitment. This new political consensus is being reinforced every day by such events as the banning of the *hijab* for Muslim girls in French schools and the virtual state of war that now exists in Algeria and Egypt between Western-backed regimes and the revolutionary Islamic movement. The war in Afghanistan, the Zionist attempts to impose 'peace' in Palestine, the slaughter of Muslims in Kashmir, and the murder and pillage of Muslims in Bosnia and Chechenia are all reinforcing the new political consensus and commitment among Muslims the world over. It is possible that what we are witnessing is the beginning of a global movement to oust the West from all Muslim countries. What is undoubtedly true is that without the Western media's attacks on the Islamic Revolution, and the undeclared war that the West is now waging against Islam in many parts of the world, it might not have been possible to achieve this level of global political consensus so quickly. The hostile Western media did for Islam something that Islam's own media, such as it is, could not achieve in so short a space of time. To pull the instincts and spiritual resources of most of the world's 1.2 billion Muslims together into a new political consensus is a service that the enemies of Islam have unwittingly performed for the object of their hate, Islam. This is something that the Quraish also did for the Prophet, upon whom be peace, and for the nascent Islam in Makkah, and later for the fledgling Islamic State in Medina. This is a process likely to continue for some time to come.

A distinctive feature of the new political consensus is that it is almost entirely revolutionary in its ethos. The idea that Islamic States could be established by winning Western-style democratic elections among competing parties has few followers among Muslims anywhere. There are few advocates of this view left, even in traditional 'democratic' Islamic parties. Democracy is now the last bastion of the hugely unpopular secular parties of the *status quo*. They have, like their colonial masters, dominated for long periods by fooling most of the people all of the time. Democracy offers them their only hope of continuing to do so, at least until Islam catches up with them. The new political consensus has thrown up many organised groups in all parts of the Muslim world who promote the idea of the Islamic Revolution in their countries and globally. These groups still have enormous problems to overcome. The chief among these is the problem of leadership. In Iran the leadership emerged from the relatively recent *usuli* tradition of *marjaiyyah*. Such a source does not exist outside the Shi'i school.

Elsewhere the leadership of the Islamic Revolution will have to emerge through political processes initiated and controlled by the Islamic movement itself. Experience in Iran, Algeria and Egypt suggests that the leadership of the revolutionary movement will have to emerge before the inevitable stage of armed conflict is reached. What is certain is that the processes involved in the shaping of the Islamic Revolution in different parts of the world will be diverse. The new Muslim political consensus is now complete in so far as the need for all parts of the world to experience Islamic Revolutions is universally accepted and understood.

The fact also is that the emergence of such a global political consensus among Muslims for the first time in history is itself an Islamic Revolution of enormous power and significance. It has set Islam on a course that should regenerate its culture, civilisation and polity. This political consensus also signals the beginning of the intellectual revolution which must precede the total and all-powerful Islamic Revolutions in all parts of the world.

NOTES:

1. The leading exponent of this view is Al-Mawardi (d. 450/1058). This issue is examined at length in Hamid Enayat, *Modern Islamic Political Thought,* London: Macmillan, 1982. On the issue of obedience to the unjust ruler, Enayat says 'generalisations about Sunni realism can be as inaccurate as those concerning Shi'i idealism: both sects have in varying degrees permitted their followers in different periods to accommodate with anomalies in the political system, whenever faced with unscrupulous rulers'. Enayat also examines the political ideas of Abu Hamid Muhammad Ghazali (d. 505/1111), Badr ad-Din Ibn Jama'ah (d. 732/1332) and Ibn Taymiyyah (d. 728/1328). Enayat's book is a rich source of material in English on the whole subject of the origin and evolution of Muslim political thought from the beginning until the modern period. Despite certain flaws, it is essential reading for those engaged in the Islamic movement whose sole or main language is English.

Chapter 5

Interim movements and partial revolutions

History does not move in leaps and bounds. Revolutions occur a long time after the development of new ideas. New ideas are first talked about among the few, then among the many, before reaching the masses. New ideas are also tried out at lower levels over long periods of time. This leads to the accumulation of experience. Gradually this builds up pressures for change. A new leadership begins to emerge. A deep sense of failure and frustration with things as they are is among the important building blocks of history. These building blocks begin to fall in place when mixed with a long history of past achievements, a prolonged sense of failure, a deep sense of loss, a strong memory of a golden era, and an even stronger sense of unfulfilled expectations. In the case of Muslims all these conditions have existed for a long time. An additional dimension of the Muslim mind and belief is an unshakeable confidence that no matter how deep their present descent into decadence may be, Islam will eventually triumph over all other cultures, ways of life, systems, theories and philosophies.

The Qur'an is firm on the issue of religious tolerance[1]. Cultural diversity has been one of the most attractive features of Islamic history and civilisation. Nevertheless, Islam's position is that all life outside Islam is rebellion against nature itself. Life in Islam alone is the normal condition or the 'state of nature'. All life must eventually return to and accept the state of nature, which is the *din* of Islam.

Given this state of mind, the Muslim worldview transcends immediate reality. Muslim political thought is situational within the framework of a transcendental view of history. The Muslim mind often overlooks or underestimates the present situation, even if it be the disastrous outcome of a war, secure in the conviction that the long-term movement of history will restore Islam's supremacy. This optimism is an integral part of the belief of all Muslims individually and of all Muslim societies collectively. Belief systems based on rationalism consider such optimism 'unrealistic' and 'irrational'. This is where the *Sirah* and the *Sunnah* of the Prophet, upon whom be peace, form a living and dynamic factor in Muslim political thought and expectations. In his lifetime, the Prophet repeatedly led his small band of the faithful in battle against overwhelming odds and won. The occasional setback or defeat was in time reversed. Such examples can no longer be dismissed as something that happened over 1400 years ago and cannot be repeated under modern conditions of large technological disparities. Islamic Iran, the victim of aggression in 1980 and facing defeat, fought on for eight years until victory on the ground and in subsequent negotiations was assured. In 1979 the Afghan *mujahidin*, faced with massive invasion and total occupation of their country by a superpower, fought an epic rearguard action lasting 10 years and won. The defeat of the Red Army in Afghanistan led directly to the disintegration of the once mighty Soviet Union that had crushed Hitler. This is the same Soviet Union and its dreaded Red Army that had held the combined might of the NATO allies at bay for half a century and matched the Americans bomb for bomb, missile for missile, ship for ship, aircraft for aircraft. The States of Eastern and Central Europe and Muslim Central Asia also owe their liberation to Islam, or the victory of the *mujahidin* in Afghanistan. A similar war is expected in Chechenia. Imam Shamyl's epic *jihad* will not have been in vain[2]. The Hizbullah drove the Israeli invaders and the American, British and French 'peace keepers' out of Lebanon. In Somalia, the dreaded US Marines were defeated and driven out by ragtag bands of fighters under 'warlords' who could not even be located by American intelligence and their ubiquitous helicopters and satellite technology. The Americans then sent in a proxy force flying the UN flag. These soldiers of imperialism drawn from such US clients as Pakistan and Bangladesh were similarly defeated and driven out. The West's defeat in Somalia is significant because it was supposed to inaugurate the 'New World Order', an euphemism for the United States' ability to dominate and impose its will on the world as the only remaining 'superpower'. The UN was to act as the US surrogate, as it had done in Korea and in the war against Iraq. This was the

48

formula that was to be the instrument for imposing the West's interests in the name of 'order', itself an euphemism for neo-colonialism, in all parts of the world.

In time the remaining Muslim areas of the former Russian Empire, Indian-occupied Kashmir and Zionist-occupied Palestine, will also be liberated. The 'national' frontiers drawn by the colonial powers to serve their interests will be abolished. For Muslims, defeat, and even prolonged occupation, however unpleasant and painful, are temporary setbacks to be reversed at some future date. Death is merely the continuation of life on another plane; death in action is the greatest reward Allah offers His devoted servants. At times pain and pleasure are one and the same thing. In a sense the enemy is an ally; he helps Muslims to struggle, wage *jihad,* and make sacrifices, including the supreme sacrifice, in the cause of Allah. A Muslim has no 'personal' or 'selfish' goals. He/she earns a living because it is necessary to sustain life which is a gift of Allah. While the pursuit of a 'good life' is positively encouraged, luxury and ostentation are frowned upon. A Muslim cannot commit suicide because that would amount to ingratitude, or the rejection of a gift from the Master and Creator. Creation, the history of creation and all that is in it, has a purpose, a Divine purpose. Man is central to that purpose[3].

It is clear that progress towards the Islamic Revolution takes time. The movement is slow but deliberate. At some stages the movement may appear to stop, go backwards, or confuse partial success with total success. It may even appear to run out of ideas. It is like someone reading a book who may stop, turn back a few pages or chapters, and read parts of them again. Running out of ideas or suffering a blank mind in the middle of writing an essay or giving a speech is a common experience. It is not altogether a bad thing. It forces the mind to dig deep into its reserves. It leads to new thinking, evaluation and integration of experience. As one set of leaders reach their optimum performance, a new set of leaders begin to emerge. A new generation with new thinkers and new leaders then plans improvements to the ideas and performance of the last generation and their leaders. The Muslim masses, too, need time to take in the lessons of recent history and prepare for the next stage of the struggle. Recent and contemporary history is very difficult to evaluate. This is partly because a large number of people who dedicated their lives to the last stage of the struggle and thought very highly of their leaders, find it difficult to accept that their ideas may have been at fault or that the leadership had made mistakes. This is because their leaders and parties have often claimed too much and had not prepared their followers for the long haul. Many of these leaders have a simplistic notion of the *Sirah* and the *Sunnah*.

They jump to the conclusion that because the Prophet's total struggle took 23 years, they too should set up the Islamic State in a similar time scale. Some have even taken the view that the struggle should now take less than 23 years because the initial phase of the conversion of individuals to Islam is not now required. Muslim countries today are already populated by vast number of Muslims. All they need is a victory at the polls, just 51 percent of the votes! In this respect the Muslim political thought that emerged during the colonial and the immediate post-colonials periods was fickle and elementary.

The processes of globalisation, the greatly revised and upgraded Muslim political thought, and the emergence of a political consensus in the wake of the Islamic Revolution in Iran are major short-term gains. In 'normal' times, in the absence of revolutionary pressures, such changes may evolve slowly over hundreds of years. Developments that might have occupied a long period of time have matured over a short period. A great deal of time has been saved. But to convert these gains into Islamic Revolutions that set up Islamic States is itself a long process. In Iran the initial breakthrough in Shi'i thought, the *usuli* revolution, occurred nearly 300 years before the full scale Islamic Revolution. It took a hundred years to establish *marjaiyyat* as a form of interim leadership. The first major trial of strength between the power of the *maraje'* and the monarchy occurred over the tobacco monopoly granted to the British in 1892, when Ayatullah Mirza Hasan Shirazi gave a *fatwa* to the effect that so long as tobacco in Iran was cultivated and distributed by the British its consumption was forbidden. The government was defeated and the monopoly collapsed. In the Constitutional Revolution (1905-11), the ulama forced the Qajar dynasty to accept an elected *majlis* to supervise the powers of the executive and the judiciary. It was another 40 years before a national government under Dr Muhammad Mussadeq nationalised the Anglo-Iranian Oil Company and the Shah was forced into exile. In 1953 the CIA carried out a coup that overthrew Dr Mussadeq and restored the Shah. In this period Ayatullah Sayyid Abul Qasim Kashani played a key role in ending British imperial power. Over the next 10 years Ayatullah Husain Burujerdi, the leading *marja'* of the time, imposed political quietism on the ulama. After his death in 1961, Ayatullah Khomeini began to defy and challenge the powers of the Shah and his parliament calling them 'illegal' and 'contrary to the Qur'an' and to the 'Iranian Constitution'. In 1963 he was arrested and sent into exile. Thus the Islamic Revolution in Iran was the culmination of changes in Shi'i theology that began more than two hundred years before. The time lag between initial 'intellectual revolution' and the ultimate overthrow of the existing order and its replacement with the Islamic State can be long; the point to note is that there had been a number of partial revolutions on the way to the total Islamic Revolution of 1979. There is a 'process' that propels the movement from the initial stirrings of the intellect among the few, to the globalisation of issues and ideas, the formalisation of a new political thought, the emergence of a consensus, a number of low level or partial achievements, and, ultimately, the bursting upon the scene of a total all-powerful, invincible Islamic Revolution that sets up the Islamic State.

This process has to be reviewed, in slow motion, frame by frame, over the entire spectrum of the history of the Islamic Revolution in Iran. Here at the Muslim Institute in London we do not have the resources to undertake such a micro study of such a complex phenomenon as the Islamic Revolution. Much of the insight we now have is from close personal contact with the Islamic Revolution, with its leaders, with the ulama, and with the intellectuals and ordinary people of Iran. But history rewards sustained loyalty. Sustained effort over a long period of historically relevant time scale is an essential dimension of the *Sirah* and the *Sunnah*. It is this dimension that is woefully absent from the framework of modern 'Islamic political parties' and the profile of the politicians they have produced. All Islamic movements that preferred the political party structure for their organisation and leadership were instantly denied the route that is prescribed and preferred by Islam. Political parties are always under pressure to produce results in the short term. Political parties are like undergraduates at universities who must achieve results within a defined time frame. The genuine, revolutionary Islamic movement, on the other hand, is under no pressure to produce results measurable on the political calendars of other parties and governments. This leads hostile observers and commentators to say that the Islamic movement is stagnant while other parties are showing political results. Even parties defeated at elections justify their participation in terms of experience gained and the opportunity given to the electorate. The Islamic movement, unlike a political party, waits for the next partial revolution that lifts it to a new level of historical change. The new level is usually followed by a period of further consolidation of new ideas, new experiences, and allows the emergence of new manpower and leadership. The period between two partial revolutions may also require the updating of ideas and their globalisation and assimilation into political thought and consensus. This is a period of preparation for the next partial or even total revolution. Nobody knows how many steps, or how many partial revolutions, there may be before the total Islamic Revolution. It is possible that the leadership goes for what it regards as a partial revolution, but the popular response and mobilisation and convergence of revolutionary forces generates enough power and momentum to produce a total Islamic Revolution. This may be what happened in Algeria in January, 1992. A political party seeking to take power through the ballot box, a strategy that the revolutionary Islamic movement would regard as a fallacy, has been forced into the role of a revolutionary movement. At the time of writing (December, 1995) the likely outcome of the armed struggle is far from clear. It would appear that the junta in Algeria might settle for a partial revolution conceding some role for FIS in the governance of the country. If FIS settled for this it would be close to what they might have achieved if the second leg of the elections had not been cancelled. The FIS leadership also has the option of taking the view that since the armed struggle has been imposed on it, they cannot now settle for anything less than a total Islamic Revolution, the dismantling of the secular State, and the installation of an Islamic State. The memory of the FLN's war of liberation from France (1954-62), which ended with the FLN accepting a colonial-style 'independence', will make it difficult for FIS to compromise this time. The people of Algeria will now demand that FIS go all the way.

The example set by the total Islamic Revolution in Iran has made it difficult for leaders elsewhere to settle for less, especially if they have already been involved in an armed struggle costing many thousands of lives. The armed struggle in Egypt, waged under the title of al-Jama'a al-Islamiyah, appears to be a classical case of an open ended armed struggle. There the Islamic movement had to be weaned away from the legacy of the moderate 'Islamic party' phase of the Ikhwan. It was Shaikh Omar Abdur Rahman, now imprisoned in America, who realised that the Ikhwan legacy could not be shaken off without armed struggle. To break the Ikhwan's party stronghold over the Islamic movement in Egypt, Shaikh Omar declared that Islam itself was a total movement, not needing a party structure or name, and that all Muslims were part of 'al-Jama'a' [the congregation] of Islam. This at once broke the Ikhwan mould and expanded the size of the Islamic movement to take in the entire Muslim population of Egypt. This has made the armed struggle in Egypt a popular struggle without frontiers, membership or even formal leadership. The al-Jama'a formula has also done away with the need for a formal political thought or even consensus. Al-Jama'a did not have to fight or formally renounce the Ikhwan's political thought or the earlier phase of the struggle. For the young fighting men of al-Jama'a everything is already present in the Qur'an and the *Sirah* and the *Sunnah* of the Prophet, upon whom be peace. This formula allows for a prolonged armed struggle without a formal leadership or arguments about organisation, control, the distribution of power, and management. So long as small bands of committed men train and fight together against the regime, described as 'enemies of Allah and instruments of Zionism and America', all other issues can be shelved for a future date when they will be decided by a *khalifah* (caliph), the ruler who will rule according to the Shari'ah and the will of Allah. In this framework of thought it is assumed that such a leader will emerge in the final stages of the struggle, just before total victory. Here again the example of the emergence of Imam Khomeini in the final stages of the struggle can be cited. The present stage of the struggle of al-Jama'a in Egypt is comparable with the struggle of the Fidaiyan-e Islam ('Devotees of Islam') in Iran during the 1950s. In Egypt the nationalist phase is behind them, thanks to the military coup of 1952 that brought Gamal Abd al-Nasser to power. There is now no other safety valve available for the Egyptian authorities to use to keep Islam at bay. The armed struggle of al-Jama'a may well turn out to be the final phase before the Islamic Revolution in Egypt.

There are many more examples of interim movements and partial revolutions in many parts of the world during the colonial period, indeed throughout history. One we need to examine in some detail is the process that unfolded in India as the Mogul Empire began to weaken and the British began to build their empire on the subcontinent. A curious fact of Muslim rule over India, which lasted eight hundred years, is that Indian Muslims somehow managed to overlook the need to develop a political thought of their own. Muslims had gone to India from outside, taking their religion, culture and language with them. Persian was the court language and the language of literature, education, poetry and high society. Hindus who wanted to play any part in matters of State, its administration, judiciary or the armed forces had to learn Persian. Muslims of India did not need a political thought because, as far as they were concerned, India did not need politics. India was under Muslim rule, and that was all that mattered. If they thought of any possible danger to the Mogul dynasty, they kept their thoughts to themselves. There was no debate, public or private, as to who or what might replace the Moguls. It was probably assumed that the fall of the Moguls was extremely unlikely but should the unthinkable happen, another Muslim dynasty would take its place. As far as they were concerned there was no need to speculate about the future, and certainly there was no need to try to develop alternative sources of political thought, institutions or Muslim power within India. Muslim power had always come to India through the Khyber Pass and, if need be, there was enough Muslim power out there that could, like water from the mountains, flow down into India again. The first man to raise the alarm of danger to Muslim rule in India was Shah Waliullah of Delhi in the middle of the eighteenth century. A renowned scholar of *hadith* (sayings of the Prophet), and one who had translated the Qur'an into Persian, Shah Waliullah wrote to the King of Afghanistan inviting him to invade India again and re-established Muslim rule there, as Mogul rule was in decline. In other words, he saw no solution within India to the problem of the decline of Muslim power. But Shah Waliullah's sons, especially Shah Abdul Aziz, carried on his work in Delhi and eventually produced the *jihad* movement that was led by Sayyid Ahmed Shahid and Sayyid Ismail Shahid. Their *jihad* movement is significant because, like all Muslims before them, they reached for the sword when in trouble. There was no tradition of seeking a political solution to a political problem. Political issues were always seen as problems of rulership or military supremacy, to be settled by military action between rival dynasties. If one of the parties was not Muslim, then *jihad*, or, more precisely *qital* (war), settled the issue. Rival claims to the throne within a dynastic family were also settled by the sword. It was a simple power-based, zero-sum, winner-take-all, model of political supremacy. Muslims had not yet learned to be politicians endlessly in search of compromise. The 'political process' works best within a system where rules are clearly laid down and enforced by law or precedence. Within the Mogul political structure there were people and groups vying for the emperor's attention, for positions of power and influence, for royal patronage, and access to the public treasury. How they went about it is not known whereas competition to fill a limited number of highly desirable positions in the State hierarchy is today regarded as the very stuff of politics. In modern political systems rivals, or rival political parties and groups, do little else. Perhaps the highly structured aristocracy that surrounded the emperor and his court did not allow for open competition for positions of power and authority. Be that as it may, the fact is that political structures, systems, procedures and rules did not exist for the peaceful transformation of one system into another. It was this that enabled the British to capture India using largely Indian soldiers. And no Muslim power flowed down the Khyber Pass.

The *jihad* movement of Sayyid Ahmed Shahid and Sayyid Ismail Shahid was in a sense also a political movement. The first thing they had to do was to raise an army and to raise funds and supplies for the army from ordinary Muslim families in northern and central India. Until then a private army raised by a group of ulama was unheard of. There was no tradition of such a movement in India. Princes and other claimants to thrones raised private armies, but not religious leaders. And the two Sayyids did not achieve all this merely to fight a local ruler; their plan was to take their army, surreptitiously, almost silently and unnoticed, across the Rajasthan desert and the Punjab, then under Sikh rule, to the rugged Pathan areas of the North-West Frontier. There they planned to establish, against local opposition if necessary, the

Islamic State headed by a *khalifah*. This Islamic State was to raise a much larger army, first to defeat Sikh power and then to march down to Delhi to dislodge the infidel British and to restore Muslim rule over India. To achieve all this they had to create a most sophisticated system of communication that kept the two Sayyids and their army supplied with weapons, money and even rations, from northern and central India. The system included fund raising, or physically collecting small contributions from a very large number of Muslim households. The cash was in heavy coins. In those days there were no banks or paper money. It was carried by convoys of camels and horses for more than a thousand miles and arrived there on time. The *jihad* movement was also perhaps the first 'political movement' on the subcontinent in so far as it depended on the support of a large number of ordinary Muslims over a large part of India. It involved the mobilisation of men and money and other resources, such as arms, horses, camels and so on. The movement ended tragically when, in 1831, the Sayyids were defeated and killed by the Sikhs at Balakot. Their organisation and movement did not survive them, but its effects may be fertilised the soil of Muslim political culture that was to respond so powerfully to a very different type of leadership and programme more than a hundred years later. The point is that even before the last of the Mogul emperors was deposed, the Muslims of India had begun their long and painful journey to politicisation. Thus the *jihad* movement must be considered a major political movement in the awakening of Indian Muslims.

While the two Sayyids were fighting and dying for Islam and Muslim political power in the North-West, another Sayyid, later to be Knighted by Queen Victoria, had entered the service of the British in Delhi as a sub-judge. The 1857 uprising against the British, styled 'the mutiny', was largely a Muslim affair, led by ulama many of whom must have been followers of the two martyred Sayyids and their *jihad* movement. This uprising was crushed by the British and led to the formal end to the Mogul Empire. During this uprising, Sayyid Ahmed Khan made a name for himself by helping to save many British lives. He now became the chief instrument of British policy towards their Muslim subjects in India. Sayyid Ahmed Khan was a complex character. His family had been in the service of Mogul emperors. Service and sycophancy came naturally to him; he was good at it.

Muslims, he said, had no choice but to become good and loyal subjects of the British. British rule was good for them because the British were more civilised than the Muslims. He persuaded the deprived and dispossessed Muslim middle classes to stop sulking over the loss of their empire and to begin to learn English and take up European mores and habits. In 1832, Macaulay had written his famous minutes on Indian education recommending that the British should create 'a class of persons, Indian in blood and colour, but English in taste, in opinions, in morals, and in intellect'[4]. Sayyid Ahmed Khan had gone to England and found that 'all good things, spiritual and worldly, which should be found in man, have been bestowed by the Almighty on Europe, and especially on England'[5]. The British helped Sir Sayyid to establish the Muhammadan Anglo-Oriental College (MAO) at Aligarh in 1875. His drive to create a class of anglophile Muslims became known as the 'Aligarh movement'. Sir Sayyid wanted 'all good things' of Europe for Indian Muslims except democracy because, if European style democratic institutions were let loose in India Muslims would become a permanent minority 'like the Irish at Westminster'. For that reason he banned Muslim participation in politics. He wanted to forge a permanent alliance between the aristocracies of the new rulers and the former rulers of India. This was necessary to keep the Hindus out of the government of India. India under Hindu rule was a nightmare scenario for the Muslim mind. But slowly the inevitable happened. The nationalist movement in India, also fanned by the British, attracted Hindus and Muslims alike. Western-educated Muslims conforming to Sir Sayyid's dreams duly emerged, but with political ideas that converged with the political aspirations of a similarly educated Hindu political elite. (Among the leading lights of this common Hindu-Muslim approach to the future of India was none other than Muhammad Ali Jinnah, later the founder of Pakistan.) This alarmed the British, who had engineered the founding of the All India Muslim League in 1906. The British, in their bid to prolong their rule over India, then played the Muslim card against the Hindus and the Hindu card against the Muslims. It was probably not Muslim awakening that broke the Hindu-Muslim political convergence; perhaps the British played a crucial role in it. Jinnah and the Muslim League merely used Islam to provide them with the necessary slogans for mass participation in the run up to Partition and Pakistan in 1947[6].

By no stretch of the imagination can Sir Sayyid's movement be called an Islamic movement, though the Sayyid was not without Islamic pretensions. Although Muslims had neglected the need to develop a political thought of their own in India, they had remained culturally close to Islam. It was Sir Sayyid who encouraged the Muslim elite to abandon Muslim culture and its two major linguistic pillars, Persian and Arabic. By persuading them to learn English, Sir Sayyid opened the doors to the wholesale importation of Western political ideas into Muslim thought. If the *jihad* movement had begun the process of evolving an Islamic political thought amongst Indian Muslims, Sir Sayyid's movement stunted and smothered its flowering. But the memory of the *jihad* movement had become a permanent part of the political culture of the Muslims of India. While the products of Sir Sayyid Ahmed Khan's Aligarh movement, organised in the Muslim League and led by men like Jinnah, were lost in the wilderness of nationalism, the deeply evocative poetry of Allama Muhammad Iqbal began to stir the Islamic roots of Muslim political culture in India. Iqbal, too, briefly toyed with Indian nationalism but soon abandoned it. Then came the Khilafat Movement in defence of the Ottoman Caliphate. This was the first popular, anti-British, Islamic movement in India. The cause of the Caliphate could not have been closer to the roots of Islam and the hearts of the Muslims of India. It produced a passing glimpse of what was possible in terms of Muslim unity and power if only a political goal within India could be defined in terms of Islam. But this was beyond the political genius of the products of the Aligarh movement. The historical process is never short of producing surprises. Iqbal's poetry had captured the imagination of the Muslim elite and masses alike. In the 1930s it was supplemented by the simple prose of Maulana Abul 'Ala Mawdoodi in Urdu, the new Muslim language of India that had, under British patronage, replaced Persian. Mawdoodi deserves to be crowned the pioneer of Islamic political thought in the subcontinent. Muslims, it seems, are not at their best in their finest hour. They produce their best when it is most needed. Mawdoodi's writings made the Qur'an and the *Sunnah* of the Prophet, upon whom be peace, relevant again. Mawdoodi could not produce an immediate political solution for what Jinnah called the 'constitutional problem' of Indian independence. But Mawdoodi cultivated the soil that had first been turned over by the *jihad* movement a hundred years before, and had more recently watered by the Khilafat Movement. Thus, when the Muslim League finally produced its constitutional cat out of the bag by demanding Pakistan, the Muslim masses were ready for it. They viewed it as a step towards an Islamic State in India itself. Mawdoodi opposed Pakistan because its leadership was secular, or not Islamic enough. He founded the Jama'at-e Islami in 1941 and talked of an 'Islamic Revolution', perhaps the first man to do so. Mawdoodi's political thought had faults which are well documented in his own writings and in commentaries by others[7]. But the importance of his contribution was recognised by Imam Khomeni himself after the Islamic Revolution in Iran nearly forty years later.

It is clear, therefore, that at different levels the pace of history is different. A movement that apparently fails at one stage may nevertheless contribute to something quite powerful and successful at a future date. In history failure at one stage may be a pre-requisite to success at another. Many interim movements and partial revolutions go to make a total Islamic Revolution. This was illustrated by the example of Iran examined above. In the case of Indian Muslims, the creation of Pakistan was a partial revolution in so far as it mobilised all Muslims under one flag in the name of Islam. But the Pakistan movement failed to meet three other criteria of a total revolution. These are: the emergence of a *muttaqi* leadership free of class or other sectional interests; the power to restructure the society as a whole at all levels; and the ability to deal with the external world on its own terms[8]. It is therefore unwise to dismiss low level movements and partial or even abortive revolutions as irrelevant; we must learn to analyse and internalise their lessons to plan or predict future course of events.

History also has a habit of producing bizarre or freakish events. Take, for example, the State of Malaysia, a totally colonial creation. The British wrote its constitution and defined it as an 'Islamic State'. How come? Roughly half the population of the new State was Chinese. With communist China hovering over them, the British did not want the Chinese in Malaysia to have a share in the political system there. In Malaysia all Muslims were also racially Malay. Thus, by defining Malaysia as an 'Islamic State', the British handed over the State to the Malays. But the Chinese controlled the country's economy. So the unwritten deal was that the Chinese would be allowed a free hand in the economy of the country and the Muslim Malays would get all the State handouts. Being constitutionally an 'Islamic State', Malaysia had to set up a whole range of 'Islamic' institutions within its racialist agenda. Whether or not this bizarre cosmetic use of Islam can contribute to eroding the secular and racialist foundations of Malaysia remains to be seen. Even such fraudulent use of Islam may generate a genuine Islamic movement that overthrows the racialist version and sets up a genuine Islamic State[9].

It is clear that events in one place and at one time can help to accelerate historical change in other places. There is also the important element of time required for new ideas and experiences to travel to other geographical, political and cultural situations. The roots of the Islamic Revolution were deep in the history of Shi'i theology. Theologians are like leaders of political parties competing for support and followers. It serves them, or their 'cause', to put as much distance as possible between their line of theology and all other theological strains within Islam. All theologians, Sunni and Shi'i, have done this to lesser or greater extent and they in turn have been exploited by whatever regimes that happened to be in power at any time. Each side invariably claims the guardianship of the whole truth, only reluctantly conceding that the other side may also have some portion of the truth on their side. Performance in terms of producing historical results, or the partial or total validation of the truth by history, is not considered a factor of importance. This is probably because sectarian theology is much easier to develop, defend and promote in a philosophical and esoteric mould than in the hothouse of history. They don't want history, or the need to change the course of history, to get in the way of their chosen path. But the Islamic Revolution in Iran, history's first total revolution in *dar al-Islam*, has forced both Shi'i and Sunni obscurantists to come to terms with actual events of great power producing results universally desired by Muslims of all schools of thought. History is like spring water or melting snow on mountains that must find its way down to the valley below. If channels are well established and merge into rivers, as is normally the case, water naturally runs into them. But if the rain or snowfall is very heavy, or of 'revolutionary' proportions, then the established channels may not be able to cope with the downpour. Though the ideas that led to the

Islamic Revolution had developed through channels established within the limited confines of Shi'i theology, Shi'i orthodoxy has proved unable to contain or manage the ideas and the power released by the Islamic Revolution. The Islamic Revolution, being a total revolution, was bound to have profound repercussions for the orthodoxy of Shi'i school. This process is still underway. But the Islamic Revolution was not only the culmination of a tradition of new thought and movement in the Shi'i tradition; it was also preceded by a large number of interim movements and partial revolutions in many parts of the vast Sunni world. These had created a whole network of channels of communication, thought, literature and political experience. But their impact on the landscape of history had been small. The channels they created had run dry. Such water as there was in them had been diverted into the hot Saudi desert. But the search for a powerful political manifestation of Islam was global. Small Islamic groups had mushroomed all over the world looking for a way out of the impasse. The post-colonial 'independence' had lost its appeal and nationalist and Islamic parties had run their course. In the meantime post-colonial migration had also created large, often vocal, Muslim minorities in Europe and North America. The first such minority to become politically active were the Algerians in France during the FLN's war of independence (1954-62). That war not only politicised the Algerians in France but also increased their numbers by fresh migration across the Mediterranean. The FLN's success spilled over its influence into Tunisia and Morocco and led to more migration into France and Spain. These minorities, inspired by the Islamic Revolution, haved played important roles in the struggles of FIS in Algeria and other similar movements in North Africa. The large Turkish community in Germany, Belgium and Holland has also developed a strong Islamic culture and political awareness; this trend among Turks living in Europe may be stronger than similar changes in Turkey itself. The emergence of Hizbullah in Lebanon acted as a conduit for the revolutionary ideas and methods of Iran into the struggle going on in Palestine. The emergence of Islamic Jihad and Hamas in Palestine are directly related to the transfer of the influence of the Islamic Revolution into this area. This direct transfer of the Iranian experience into some parts of the Islamic movement elsewhere was inevitable and natural. Some results, such as the 1982 defeat of Israel in Lebanon, were spectacular.

However, absorbing the ideas, methods and power of the Islamic Revolution in its raw form was not easy. A number of difficulties were in the way. For instance, there was no sympathetic media reporting the Islamic Revolution while Iran's own newspapers, magazines and news agencies were of poor quality. Most of the revolutionary rhetoric originating in Iran was in Farsi and wrapped in Shi'i terminology, even insensitive theology originating in the Safavid era. Some daily newspapers in English, printed in Iran for overseas circulation, carried pages of reprints from Shi'i texts. On top of all this was Western propaganda which consisted mostly of blatant lies. The hostile propaganda and the lack of sophistication in Iran's own presentation of the total revolution could not hide the essential facts; these were the obvious and effective power of the Islamic Revolution and the modesty, simplicity and piety *(taqwa)* of its leadership. And of course the additional dimension that could not be hidden from Muslim eyes worldwide was the spectacular success of the Islamic Revolution against powers that had been declared enemies of Islam throughout history.

It was therefore inevitable that the Islamic Revolution would have a great impact on the Muslim mind everywhere. Its impact was greater on individuals and low level Islamic organisations that had been struggling for long periods of time without much to show for their efforts and sacrifices. These grassroots movements were greatly inspired by the Islamic Revolution. But the great 'Islamic parties' of this century such as the Jama'at-e Islami in Pakistan, India and Bangladesh and the Ikhwan al-Muslimoon in Arab countries found it difficult to absorb the lessons of the Islamic Revolution. Their 'political thought' and financial links proved as narrow and resistant to new ideas as any deviant theology. They, like all modern politicians, were not concerned with right or wrong, or even historical evidence of results achieved; their concern was their short term interests and commitments made to such regimes as those of Saudi Arabia. Nonetheless, large numbers of 'Islamic workers' and 'Islamic leaders' made a beeline to Tehran to see Imam Khomeini and to express their support for the Islamic Revolution. Hundreds, perhaps thousands, were also invited to Iran to the first few anniversaries of the Revolution. Imam Khomeini, in his annual messages to the *hujjaj,* stressed the unity of the Ummah, insisting that those who talked of Shi'i and Sunni differences were neither Shi'i nor Sunni. But these incantations from the Imam seemed to have little impact on Iranian ulama who travelled the world ostensibly explaining the Islamic Revolution. Their vocabulary, style and presentation was almost without exception Shi'i. Also, Iranian cultural centres and embassies overseas made little attempt to establish meaningful relationships with Sunni Muslims. Their cultural and religious activities have remained largely confined to the local Shi'i communities. At the same time the Saudi/US alliance against the Islamic Revolution began to pump enormous new resources into 'Islamic parties' and groups that had been traditionally friendly to them. The most important of these were of course the Ikhwan and the Jama'at-e Islami on the subcontinent and the Arab world and their offshoots in Europe and North America. The Ikhwan and Jama'at leaders who had gone to Tehran in the wake of the Islamic Revolution to proclaim their support, soon found flimsy grounds on which to turn against Iran. They also accused Iran of refusing to make peace with a 'brotherly Muslim country, Iraq'.

Few people outside Iran, and not many within Iran, understood that the Islamic Revolution had originated in an intellectual revolution in the Shi'i tradition. The phrase that caused great confusion was that Iran wanted to 'export the revolution'. The opponents of the Islamic Revolution outside Iran turned this to mean that this would amount to a form of Iranian/Shi'i colonial empire in the name of Islam. In these circumstances the task of explaining the Islamic Revolution to a wider audience outside Iran was a difficult one. Groups who stuck to this task were largely those who were engaged in struggles of their own, especially in Lebanon and Palestine. The Islamic Revolution also had its impact on movements in Algeria, Egypt, Afghanistan and Kashmir. Almost none of the universities in Muslim countries took up the task of researching and writing about the Islamic Revolution. Among the handful of private and poorly resourced institutions that took up the challenge was the fledgling Muslim Institute for Research and Planning in London. Across the Atlantic in Toronto a small newsmagazine, the *Crescent International,* published since 1973 from the basement of Latif and Zahida Owaisi[10], turned itself into a mouthpiece of the Islamic Revolution. The Muslim Institute and the *Crescent International* had been independently developing similar ideas before the Islamic Revolution in Iran. After the Islamic

Revolution they began to convert the news from Iran into the commonly understood language of political rhetoric and debate.

For the Institute this was a short-term expedience while they tried to develop a better understanding of what had happened and was happening in Iran. This was to have an impact on Iran itself of which the Muslim Institute was quite unaware. In Iran not everybody caught up in the Islamic Revolution was very religious or grasped the underlying currents of Shi'i thought. Among them were many academics, writers, journalists and broadcasters. They, too, were having a hard time of it. For them the output from London and Toronto was a blessing. They began to translate this material, conveniently written in newspaper length articles, into Farsi. It was published in daily newspapers and in the hundreds of revolutionary magazines that were published in Iran at this time. While the Muslim Institute's high-pitched non-Irani and non-Shi'i interpretation of the Revolution was being fed into Iran, the Muslim Institute also began to acquire a deeper understanding of what was going on.

The Muslim Institute had realised very early on that in the long-term its relationship with the Islamic Revolution, the new Islamic State and its leadership, would depend on how much political support they gave to Iran when Iran was under attack from all sides, rather than on their understanding, or lack of it, of the finer points of Shi'i theology. Imam Khomeini's repeated pronouncements on the unity of all Muslims was a great encouragement. The Muslim Institute and the *Crescent International* focussed on all the enemies of the Islamic Revolution, in particular the Americans, the Saudis and of course the Ba'athist regime of Saddam Hussain that had invaded Iran. Their speakers travelled the world talking about the Islamic Revolution, preparing the ground for the acceptance of a new political thought originating in the Islamic Revolution. This, in their view, was essential for the regeneration of the global power of Islam. There was no shortage of Muslim audiences to hear this bold and upbeat message. They became household names in Iran and in many parts of the world. In this process a great many ideas, revolutionary methods and political attitudes were transferred from Iran to Muslims outside, and a great many ideas and concerns of Muslims outside Iran were heard in Iran. During this critical period the Muslim Institute served as a two-way

64

conduit. Its standing in Iran was based on its total and unquestioning political support for the Islamic Revolution against all its enemies. Outside Iran the Muslim Institute had an audience because Muslims had been without a significant victory against their enemies for hundreds of years and were prepared, indeed eager, to accept the victory of the Islamic Revolution as their own.

The Muslim Institute also contributed in another important process that was underway in all parts of the Muslim world. In the aftermath of the Islamic Revolution, the Americans, the Saudis and their allies throughout the world tried to isolate Iran from the bulk of the Ummah by branding it Shi'i. There were occasions in the 1980s when the Ummah might have split right down the middle along its Shi'i/Sunni fault line. But the ideas promoting the underlying unity of the Ummah as part of a global Islamic movement proved too strong for them to overcome.

Then came the publication of *The Satanic Verses*, the global Muslim outcry against it, and Imam Khomeini's *fatwa* sentencing its author to death. London was the eye of the storm, tailor made for the Muslim Institute's political skills. The defence of the *fatwa*, too, fell to the Muslim Insitute, though many others played significant roles. The fact that the British could not silence or punish Muslims on their own soil took a great deal of pressure off Iran. For the Muslim Institute the *fatwa*, too, could not be branded a Shi'i pronouncement. And once again the unity of the Ummah, and of all schools of thought in Islam, was uniquely demonstrated for the whole world to see. Equally, the West's unified position against Islam was exposed in a way that perhaps nothing else could have done. The timing of the publication of *The Satanic Verses* and the Imam's *fatwa* was impeccable in terms of history. The Soviet Union had just been driven out of Afghanistan and was beginning to unravel. The West was putting on a show of triumphalism. But the party celebrating the West's total triumph over all hostile forces in the world was spoiled by the *fatwa* and its unanimous endorsement by Muslim public opinion all over the world.

The founding of the Muslim Institute in London in 1971-72 was a shot in the dark, comparable with Columbus sailing west hoping to reach India. In the 1980s, the Muslim Institute was among those in the Muslim world who took the Islamic Revolution on board. This unexpected thunderbolt of history helped to validate much of the political thought of the Muslim Institute. The 'Satanic Verses' *fatwa* and its aftermath then created a transforming historical situation for Muslims in the West. The Muslim Institute now had the opportunity to take full advantage of it by extending its derivative political thought in new directions. This it did by developing ideas on which Muslim minorities in the West could build political structures of their own. The two crucial papers that the Muslim Institute wrote and published were *Generating Power Without Politics* (1990) and *The Muslim Manifesto* (1990). These became the intellectual foundations on which The Muslim Parliament of Great Britain was put together and launched in January 1992. The Muslim Parliament as a structure is in an embryonic stage. It has to go through the processes of early struggles for survival, then build up a record of movement and achievement leading to stability and the ability to generate its own power. Taken together, the early ideas of the Muslim Institute, their historical validation within the framework of the Islamic Revolution, the successful defiance of the West over the *fatwa*, and the founding of the Muslim Parliament of Great Britain amount to an interim movement and partial revolution of considerable significance for the future.

All instances of interim movements and partial revolutions examined in this chapter have contributed to the on-going intellectual revolution, the process of globalisation, the development of Muslim political thought, and the evolution of a worldwide political consensus among Muslims. All these processes working in tandem at a time of a transforming historical situation is a new phenomenon in the history of Islam. It is a situation to fill the hearts of Muslims with hope of even greater achievements and possibilities, while it will depress the enemies of Islam and Muslims and make them fight harder against us. The process that converts low-level movements into power and achievement, generating more power, is examined in the next chapter.

NOTES:

1. Qur'an 109:1-6.

2. Lesley Blanch, *The Sabres of Paradise,* New York: Carrol and Graf, 1984.

3. For the Almighty's view of man, see the Qur'an, especially *ayas* 2:30; 6:165; 4:1-36; 17:23-39; 29:8-9; 30:38; 31:33; 46:15; 70:22-35; 6:60,72; 10:45-46; 6:164; 10:99; 17:11,13,71; 22:5; 23:12-14; 40:67; 90:4,8-10; 92:4-11; and 95:4.

4. Michael Edwards, *Raj,* London: Pan Books, 1969, p 70.

5. Cited in G. F. I. Graham, *The Life and Works of Sayyid Ahmed Khan,* London: Hodder and Stoughton, 1909, p 127.

6. For a detailed treatment of these events, see Kalim Siddiqui, *Conflict, Crisis and War in Pakistan,* London: Macmillan, 1972, pp 7-47.

7. See, for example, Kalim Siddiqui's paper 'Muslim Political Thought and Behaviour under Colonialism', in Kalim Siddiqui (ed), *Issues in the Islamic Movement 1985-86,* London and Toronto: The Open Press, 1982, p 192.

8. See a definition of the Islamic Revolution in *Issues in the Islamic Movement,* London and Toronto: The Open Press, 1982, p 192.

9. The author has visited Malaysia on a number of occasions. During a visit in 1994, he was told by usually reliable sources that the British version of Islam and Malay nationalism was losing ground and a genuine Islamic movement was beginning to take shape.

10. Zahida died of cancer on September 13, 1995. Despite her duties as a mother of two young sons, she worked day and night typesetting for *The Crescent International* during its early years.

Chapter 6

Movement, power and achievement

Political systems are complex systems. They have long memories and rely on past experiences. For example, the memory of the French Revolution affects all French political behaviour to this day. If something has happened in the past it is likely to happen again in the future. This is another way of saying that history repeats itself. In a loving relationship past patterns of contact are repeated frequently. If two parties have fought over an issue in the past, they expect, or fear, that they would, given the chance, fight again. The relationship between Germany and its European neighbours is of this kind. Most Europeans suspect German motives in the European Union. Right-wing politicians throughout Europe suspect that Germany is building a European empire through means other than war.

If we want to predict what someone is likely to do in the future we look into his/her past, something we often call a person's 'character'. Some political systems are aggressively goal-achieving, for example the modern States of Israel, the United States, Britain, Germany, Japan, France and Russia. In each case there is a tradition of violence at crucial times in the country's history. In this list three, Israel, the US and Germany, were created through violence and war. Their 'finest hour' is violent. Periodic violence and wars are their systemic needs. They must pick a fight every so often and appear to win in order to sustain their self-image. Britain, France and Russia were large colonial powers. They had created their empires by war. They, too, feel good when fighting and winning, especially outside Europe and preferably against Muslims. For goal-achieving political systems their memory, or selective and self-glorifying history, plays the same role as axioms do in scientific inquiry. These axioms are self-evident truths. No truth can maintain its position as the truth unless it be repeatedly validated.

This validation of the truth takes many shapes and forms. A biological system often regards its reproductive function as its greatest achievement. A political system validates its internal or domestic legitimacy as well as its performance in relation to other similar systems in the world system. A scientist working with a set of axioms makes progress and believes that his successes validate the axioms. But it can happen, indeed does frequently happen, that results of scientific experiments build up anomalies that begin to question the validity of the axioms themselves. Newton's ideas in physics remained dominant for nearly 300 years before Einstein. In other words, scientific truths are only true for as long as their validity is not successfully challenged. When challenged, the self-evident truth of the former paradigm becomes volatile and changeable and new axioms take over until they in their turn are challenged and displaced from their position on the pedestal. Historically demonstrable results are the very essence of any truth: no results, no truth.

Most political systems are movements of one kind or another. They try to move forward in a ceaseless drive to attain political goals. They often try to represent their routine movement as their 'output' because actual achievements are hard to come by. The fuel that propels political systems is power. A system needs initial power to get going. Having to push a car to get it started is a common experience. The system's initial movement provided by external push begins to generate its own power for the next stage. Eventually the system's forward movement over a long period of time leads to achievements. Achievements generate more power more quickly than routine movement. Achievements also enhance the power generating capacity of the system. A great achievement can also provide surplus power to be put aside for later use. This is like having a savings account or credit balance of unused or available power. Achievements may also increase the size of the system. More power, sometimes called greater capacity, leads the system to set higher goals or targets. Political systems perceive power as a fluid commodity: if it be not going up it must be going down. They therefore engage in a great deal of wasteful activity designed, or so they would have us believe, to acquire more power. Buying more armaments of latest design and capacity is one such activity. In the long run this type of activity often depletes their power and resource base.

It is possible to look at Islam as a political system. The English word 'religion' does not adequately define or describe Islam. It has led to much confusion and unjustified comparison of Islam with other 'religions'. The entire *Sirah* of the Prophet, upon whom be peace, may be viewed as that of an architect building a political system. At its inception in Makkah, Islam had no power, only a few Divine axioms revealed to the Prophet, upon whom be peace. The Prophet invited those closest to him to accept these axioms and to build a system around them with himself at its centre. Thus the natural progression of the system is in this order: first the Leader, then a body of axioms, then a few followers to form the nucleus of the new system. Initially the system had no power of its own. Its power was borrowed from tribal and familial links that the Prophet had before being called to prophethood. At one stage he even sought protection for his followers from the Negus, king of neighbouring Ethiopia, across the Red Sea. Similarly, when the Quraish of Makkah imposed an economic boycott of Muslims, it was the Prophet's position as a member of the Banu Hashim clan that helped them survive and finally break the boycott. For 13 years the fledgling Islamic political system, consisting of the Leader, some revealed axioms, and a handful of followers, was pitted against the combined might of the Quraishite tribes in Makkah and its environs. During this period the political system of Islam had no territory, though the Prophet made many journeys outside Makkah to try to find allies. His trip to Ta'if is the most famous of these excursions. There he was insulted and abused and expelled, but he refused to curse his tormentors on the ground that perhaps their children would one day come into the fold of Islam.

Guided by an *ayah* in the Qur'an[1], the Prophet set about looking for help from an established source of power outside Makkah. Over three years the Prophet carried out most delicate and secret negotiations with al-'Aws and al-Khazraj, two tribes from Yathrib. This led to a rapid increase in the number of Muslims in Yathrib and the Prophet concluded two covenants with them in successive years. These are known in history as the Covenants of 'Aqabah, 'Aqabah being the name of a place just outside Makkah where they met. The first Covenant, between the Prophet and 12 men from Yathrib, was little more than a general declaration of common moral values they would uphold. In it the 12 agreed to adhere to the absolute unity of God, neither to steal nor to commit adultery, neither to kill their [female] children nor knowingly commit any evil, and not to fail to obey God in His commandment of any good[2]. The Prophet sent one of his companions to Yathrib to teach them the Qur'an and to explain Islam to them. The following year 73 men and two women came to Makkah and concluded a second Covenant of 'Aqabah with the Prophet. This was an outright political and military pact that extended unqualified protection for the Prophet against his enemies. Slowly, in ones and twos, most Muslims left Makkah and took up residence in Yathrib. The Muslim community in Yathrib steadily grew in numbers through local conversion and migration from Makkah until they became a substantial power there. Now the Prophet had a territorial base and dependable allies outside Makkah. Then came Allah's permission for the Prophet to migrate to Yathrib as well. With the Prophet's arrival there, Yathrib became known as *Medinatun Nabi,* or the City of the Prophet, or just Medina.

For thirteen years in Makkah Islam had been a political system without a territory. The absence of a territorial base did not prevent Islam in Makkah from undertaking negotiations with its friends and enemies, organising migration and entering into agreement with the Negus of Ethiopia. In Makkah Islam also suffered an economic blockade, sought allies outside Makkah, and negotiated and concluded the two Covenants of 'Aqabah. At no time in Makkah did the Prophet say, and the Qur'an was still coming in short *surahs* and *ayahs,* that Muslims would one day seek a territory. But it was understood. In Makkah the Prophet's companions, the *sahabah,* were placing and taking bets on when the Byzantine and Persian empires would fall to Islam! They knew that the Makkan crucible was only a preparatory period for supreme power and statehood.

In Medina the Prophet immediately set about consolidating the power of Islam, sending armed expeditions to harass the trading caravans of Quraish, which passed through the narrow land corridor between Medina and the Red Sea on their way to or from Syria. These expeditions were designed to weaken the power of the Makkans, who might be thinking of invading Medina. In today's strategic thinking, these were pre-emptive expeditions. The Makkans were indeed thinking of invading Medina to destroy this fledgling base of Islam before it became too strong for them to deal with. This led to the Battle of Badr in the second year of the Hijra. A party of just over 300 Muslims, led by the Prophet himself, who had set out to intercept a caravan, ended up fighting the full might of the noblemen of Quraish of Makkah numbering over 1000. And they won! Badr was the turning point when Islam came of age as a political and military power in Arabia, perhaps in the world for all time to come. One does not need to go over all the 68 military expeditions that the Prophet launched from Medina to prove that the Prophet was no mere religious preacher. In Makkah he was a statesman without a State. In Medina he became a statesman with a small territorial State that he went on to extend until it included not only Makkah but most of the Arabian peninsula. Territorial expansion, however, was incidental to the main purpose. The Prophet totally transformed the values by which the people lived and died. He changed their social and economic structures and their outlook. The State merely provided the framework within which a new society was created and flourished. The State in Islam is an act of faith and duty, not an act of common consent of its citizens.

Islam does not create a total functional system because it has the best theology. The totality of Islam is more than its theology, it includes the historical performance of the system it creates. If results do not follow as they did when the method of Islam was first applied, then there is something wrong with the application. A goal-achieving system must achieve goals or lose power and slowly weaken to a point where others will defeat and destroy it. This is precisely what has happened to Islam as a result of error and deviance on the part of Muslim rulers, beginning with the conversion of *khilafah* into *malukiyyah* by the Umaiyyads. The subsequent emergence of rival man-made theologies has damaged the regenerating powers of Islam. In the Shi'i school it took three hundred years for the *usuli* method of *ijtihad* to correct their deviation before they could establish the Islamic State in Iran. Although the *usuli* movement has made great progress, it still has some way to go before it can claim to have offered a common agenda for all Muslims. This is a gap that has to be filled and Iran is well placed to do so. In the Sunni school there is as yet no sign of a comparable corrective process at work. The works of Mawdoodi and

Hasan al-Banna were at best early stirrings of change. Sayyid Qutb lifted Muslim political thought many notches and provided some badly needed new insights. His influence on the Islamic movement everywhere, including Iran, has been profound. In Iran itself, Ali Shari'ati helped to prepare western-educated youth to accept the leadership of the ulama.

One important difference between movement and achievement should be noted. The movement transmits ideas across frontiers. Frontiers have never been able to stop the movement of ideas. But ideas which are backed up by concrete achievements travel faster and are more effective. This is the meaning of the proverb 'nothing succeeds like success'. This is why the achievements of the Islamic Revolution in Iran have become globalised so quickly. This is also why the Saudi/US lobby, assisted by the Jama'at/Ikhwan duopoly, has had such a hard time branding it a Shi'i revolution of no or little relevance to the Sunni world. The prevailing world system is of course entirely opposed to the Islamic Revolution in Iran, and the methods employed in Iran to establish a bridgehead across the sea of corruption, oppression and cultural decline that are integral parts of the world system. The world system's reaction to the Islamic Revolution is the reaction of an enemy that finds that the opposing side has established a bridgehead on its territory. This bridgehead of Islam on Iranian territory, previously controlled by the United States, was immediately attacked with military invasion, economic sanctions, diplomatic boycott and a ceaseless propaganda war. This propaganda war has been extended to include all of Islam and the political expression of Islam anywhere in the world. Even schoolgirls wearing headscarves are perceived as a threat to the dominance of Western culture and civilisation. This is because the headscarf is now seen as part of a successful relaunching of the power of Islam against the world system. The West has seen women in scarves bring down their favourite ruler, the Shah of Iran. Muslim women in *hijab,* walking down the streets of cities in Europe and America, are viewed as political slogans against the West's claims to have liberated and emancipated women. It is the initial victory of the Islamic Revolution in Iran that has given new confidence to Muslim women throughout the world.

Once concrete achievements begin to fuel the movement, the

movement feels greater power flowing into its system. The global Islamic movement in particular claims a legitimacy greater than that of a State. The modern nation-States are the building blocks of the world system that is dominated by the West. Once a global Islamic movement acquires global following and legitimacy, all States whose statehood is predicated on nationality may be considered under sentence of disintegration and death. The grafting of nationalism on Islam, or Islam on nationalism, is an operation impossibe to perform. They are mutually irreconcilable. The attempts by secular, post-colonial leaders to achieve this goal is at the root of most of the instability and turmoil that is found in Muslim countries today. The global Islamic movement is an alternative world system. The existing world system has run out of steam and ideas. The axioms of the Western civilisation are under attack. These axioms are not based on any Divine source. They do not have and cannot claim to have eternal validation or truth as their foundation. They can only claim 'scientific' and historical validity. Karl Marx also claimed as much. The collapse of marxism as a philosophy and communism as a 'scientific system' have in fact, in the long term, also destroyed the foundations of the Western civilisation itself. The Western civilisation now has no validity beyond its ephemeral achievements. The achievements of the West are no longer qualitative; they are entirely quantitative. These amount to economic growth, levels of consumption, rates of inflation, technology and the 'feel good factor' in opinion polls. Such scientific and technological progress that the West has to its credit is just as likely to prove them wrong. This is because the West has used its scientific and technological progress largely as instruments for the oppression and exploitation of the greater part of mankind. In the long term even the 'feel good factor' of Western man may not be enough to compete with the feel good factor that Islam has to offer mankind. The Muslim woman in *hijab* in the West almost certainly has a higher 'feel good' level than most scantily dressed Western women. Women whose lives are dotted with temporary 'relationships', one-night stands, unwanted pregnancies, a string of abortions or illegitimate births, cannot have a high 'feel good' level. Much the same applies to men. Happiness is not merely a life of endless parties, drinking, adultery, holidays, relationships, travel, tranquilisers, and income, savings, pensions, insurance policies, mortgages, and healthy bank accounts. Today Islam alone produces the complete good person,

74

totally satisfied and happy with their relationship with their Creator and the Creator of all things. Consumerism as a basis of happiness is a flimsy foundation even for individuals, let alone a whole civilisation and the world system.

Once the transformation of values and outlook is added to the achievements of a system, the system becomes invincible. Real power lies in faith, belief, contentment, commitment, responsibility and accountability to the Almighty in the Hereafter. Real power does not mean the ability to march or fly large numbers of troops to distant lands and drop bombs on civilian populations. Had that been the case the Red Army would have won in Afghanistan and the Soviet Union would have held together; the United States would not have lost in Vietnam and would not have had to stage humiliating withdrawals from Lebanon and Somalia. Real power is the ability to overcome overwhelming odds as the *mujahidin* in Afghanistan have done, as the people of Vietnam did, as the Hizbullah did in defeating the Israelis, and as the Somalies did in forcing the US and its UN proxies out of their country. Thus, in a sense, the coercive power of the superpowers is of limited value. In conditions where weak opposition remains defiant, such power can be a liability. If it is used it might get beaten, if it is not used its credibility is lost. Military power is merely an instrument, which may or may not work. Any instrument depends on the skill and legitimacy of the user. Most modern political leaders and holders of high office have doubtful moral foundations to their authority. All they usually have is a man-made constitution and a spurious, even contentious, national interests. Even their professional soldiers have little more than pride in their professionalism to drive them forward. They will only fight so long as the chances of being killed are not significantly greater than being run over by a bus in civilian life. Once the count of body bags builds up, the pressure to withdraw and send in proxy Pakistanis and Bengladeshis or others in blue berets builds up. This is not power, it is a mockery of power. This type of power cannot guarantee the survival of any State, or group of States, that arrogates to itself the claim to being the ultimate civilisation. Western civilisation is a castle built on sand.

Real power is neither offensive nor defensive. Real power is regenerative; it is power to recover from defeat and dismemberment. This is a test that the Western civilisation has not so far faced. As civilisations go, the West is only a stripling. The defeat of Nazism and Fascism, and the collapse of communism, do not amount to the end of the West's internal contradictions. Such values as the West claims to have, e.g. freedom, human rights, self-determination, democracy etc., it is afraid to uphold even in its own backyards such as Bosnia and Chechenia. The West actively opposes the globalisation of its own values because that would mean the end of its hegemony over large areas of the world and control over resources. The triumph of the West is a hollow slogan. In fact the capitalist and free-market economies are themselves in crisis. They have celebrated the collapse of communism as their victory; in fact, it was their defeat as well. The Soviet Union was not far from reaching the *nirvana* of consumerism. Western consumerism as a civilisation cannot last for long because for its survival and growth it depends on a permanently unequal relationship between the producers of raw materials and commodities of Asia, Africa and South America on the one hand and the heartland of the West in Europe and North America on the other. No civilisation that cannot do justice to all its parts can be called, or can claim to be, global. The West is global in much the same way as the AIDS virus is global. Most parts of the world are suffering from the domination that the West has acquired over their markets, resources, and even political systems. This is banditry, not civilisation. And bandits' domination and occupation usually lasts a very short time in historical terms. This is why the era of direct European colonialism was relatively short and the era of neo-colonialism is unlikely to be significantly longer. The deliberate and wanton destruction of traditional societies that the West has carried out has also destroyed the values that might one day have helped the West itself to recover from self-inflicted wounds[3].

Islam on the other hand has faced, and is currently facing, the crisis of having to recover from the near total destruction of all its structures and trappings of power. We must distinguish here between the power that resides in structures and the power of faith, belief, contentment, certainty, commitment, responsibility and accountability to the Almighty. Power of the structures is destructible while the power of values is indestructible and eternal. It is the power of eternal values that underpins the power of the structures. Structures can be destroyed by enemy action, or weaken and collapse through internal error and deviation in terms of the core values. We are back once again to the familiar refrain of this study, that it is the progressive deviation of Muslim rule from Islam's core values that led to internal weakness which invited invasion from without. Attempts have been made to superimpose man-made theology, or theological justifications, on the core values. No school of thought in Islam has prospered in terms of its secondary, superimposed theology. In the Shi'i school the *usuli* revolution was an attempt to correct some of the excesses of the *akhbari* position. This on-going corrective process over two hundred years has brought them to the Islamic Revolution. Imam Khomeini's *ijtihad* made major changes to traditional Shi'i positions on issues of leadership, State and politics. This corrective process continues.

This is the real power of Islam. The destruction of structures is a temporary loss, which leaves the regenerative powers of Islam unaffected. The first step in the regenerative process is an intellectual revolution. It is possible for a number of interim movements and partial revolutions to add up to an intellectual revolution of sufficient power to generate a total Islamic Revolution. It is more than likely that the processes of globalisation, the emergence of a vibrant Muslim political thought and the rapidly evolving global consensus do in fact add up to an intellectual revolution of strength sufficient to support Islamic Revolutions in many parts of the world. We can not know this until the outcome of partial revolutions that are now in progress or in the pipeline be known. The outcome of the struggles now underway in Algeria and Egypt should tell us a great deal about the likely course of events in the future in many parts of the world.

Military victory normally means greatly enhanced political power. But this has not happened in Afghanistan. This is largely because the war against the Soviet occupation of the country was not conducted by a unified political system of Islam. All parts of the country instinctively rose up against the Soviet occupation. The *jihad* was conducted on the basis of the local tribal structures of traditional Afghan society. The authority of the nation-State was restricted to Kabul and a few of the larger cities. The nation-State had been captured by the Soviet Union even before the Red Army marched in;

indeed, the Red Army was 'invited' by the government in Kabul. The war was between the Red Army laden with high technology, including air power, and the hand-held weapons carried by the *mujahidin*. The *mujahidin* won. But external intervention ensured that their victory would not be converted into a political system above the tribal level. Hence the civil war at two levels - between tribal warlords, and between Islamic groups and those who want to return to the secular nation-State structure as before. Whether or not an Islamic movement can emerge out of this anarchy remains to be seen. The example of Afghanistan shows that it may be dangerous to achieve too much without order, structures and leadership. In neighbouring Pakistan a similar situation has existed for many years. There has existed anarchy, chaos, disorder and low level civil war in many parts of the country. At the same time there are many religious parties and ritualised religious practices are observed by the majority of the people. Common wisdom in the country has it that what Pakistan needs is an 'Islamic Revolution like Iran' or 'this country needs a Khomeini'.

NOTES:

1. Qur'an 17:8.

2. Muhammad Husayn Haykal, *The Life of Muhammad,* North American Trust Publications, 1976, p 154.

3. See Kalim Siddiqui's paper, 'Integration and Disintegration in the Politics of Islam and Kufr', in Kalim Siddiqui, *Issues in the Islamic Movement 1982-83,* London and Toronto: The Open Press, 1984, pp 1-27.

Chapter 7

The Islamic Revolution and the Islamic State

So far in this study we have referred to the Islamic Revolution without defining it, though a definition formulated in 1980 has been quoted in chapter five. Our emphasis has been on the conditions that must exist before a country is likely to generate and experience the liberating power of what is now called the Islamic Revolution. The Islamic Revolution, like any revolution, is an event. It may also be described as a compound of many related events taking place simultaneously at all levels of a society. The Islamic Revolution is that point in time when changes in the outlook, values and preferences of a people, assiduously brought about over a long period of time, suddenly change their collective behaviour as well. The mood of the populace demands and secures total change in the values of the society, its structure and leadership. The old order is destroyed and a new order is established. The destruction of the old order is important, otherwise its germs may survive and penetrate the new order and seek to destroy it from within. Leadership must change hands totally and irrevocably. New institutions are created to define and defend the new values of the society. The collective effect of all these changes are consolidated in the structure of the Islamic State. The head of the Islamic State must be a leader who exercises authority delegated to him by Allah *(subhanahu wa ta'ala)* through the Prophet, upon whom be peace. The Islamic Revolution is that point in time when all the elements that go to make the Islamic State come together and the Islamic State is set up. The Islamic Revolution is the mother of the Islamic State. The Islamic State is the infant that is born of the Islamic Revolution. The Islamic Revolution is the public expression and consummation of the power of a people that is necessary to establish the Islamic State. This power is the power of the Islamic Revolution. This power, and the blood of the masses spilled by the old order in its

79

dying days, legitimise the child, the Islamic State. At its birth, the Islamic State is protected by its mother, the Islamic Revolution. Some of the power of the Islamic Revolution must become internalised in the structure or body of the Islamic State. The Islamic Revolution, like a bolt of lightning, is a moment in time that passes. But while it lasts it illuminates many dark corners of history and, for the perceptive, the present and the future. The Islamic State is the new structure that shall remain, grow and multiply. For a period of time the Islamic State must be protected by the power of the Islamic Revolution. But, ultimately, the Islamic State must stand on its own feet; it must develop its own power from its own resources, performance, movement and achievement.

In this framework we must examine the performance of the only Islamic Revolution and the Islamic State of which we have direct and contemporary experience. On the face of it the destruction of the old order was total and complete. The monarchy was abolished and most of its loyal servants went into exile. A Revolutionary Council took over the government of Iran and drafted an entirely new Constitution. The mobilised power of the masses under the new leadership was so great that it proved invincible. It is difficult to recall another revolution in history where the power available to the new revolutionary leadership was as great as the power at the disposal of the leaders of the Islamic Revolution in Iran. The question then arises as to whether or not the leadership used this power wisely and to the full extent of its potential? We are too close to the event to attempt a definitive answer to this question. Historians yet unborn may search for an answer. We don't know, for instance, what options were considered by the Revolutionary Council and presented to the Imam. We don't know why certain choices were made. What were the limits, if any, real or perceived, to the leadership's power and capacity to govern? What was the spectrum of opinion within the Revolutionary Council? Did the Imam impose his preferences or did he have to seek a balance or consensus? Did he have to take such factors into account? We know, for example, that on such issues as land reform there was an impasse between the elected *majlis* (parliament), and the Council of Guardians. The Imam had constitutional and popular authority to break the deadlock but chose not to. The bill to carry out radical land reforms that was passed by the *majlis* was lost. Did this save the feudal aristocracy? What influence did the aristocracy have on the ulama who blocked the bill? Has the failure to carry out meaningful land reforms permanently restricted the power of the leadership in the future? What are the long-term implications of this for the quality of life in the Islamic State of Iran and its moral and structural foundations?

We have already noted the long sequel of 'partial revolutions' within the Shi'i school that occurred over two hundred years before the full scale Islamic Revolution was possible. It is also possible that the Islamic Revolution that created the Islamic State in 1979 was itself an incomplete process. A number of new 'partial revolutions' may be required to correct or complete some of the unfinished business of the Islamic Revolution. Perhaps the young ulama trained after the Islamic Revolution will demand the abolition of the landed aristocracy in a way their elders could not or would not. A future *majlis* may pass another bill to secure extensive land reforms and it may not be opposed by a future Council of Guardians. It is also possible that there were many other measures that should have been taken but were not taken because of limits of power or perception in the leadership. This unfinished business, now lying dormant, may slowly return to the active agenda of the leadership and government in Iran. The composition of a future *majlis* may force these issues back on to the agenda. There is no political system that does not experience a healthy competition for leadership. The new political system in Iran is unlikely to be an exception. New leaders need new ideas. Their search for new ideas may revive the deferred agenda and the unfinished business of the Islamic Revolution. In fact it is important that this should happen. Going back to the Islamic Revolution for new ideas will extend the life and influence of the Islamic Revolution and give strength to the Islamic State. It is also good that there should be a competition for new ideas among the new and aspiring leadership of the future. The greater the competition for new ideas, the better will be the quality of leadership that emerges. Failure in certain key areas, such as the economy, may force a search for new ideas, new policies, and new men. However, the processes and procedures of this competition should evolve within the moral framework of Islam. Under no circumstances should they try to emulate the two-party or multi-party politics of modern democracies. Opposition for the sake of opposition must not become the norm or habit of the system.

It is widely known and recognised that many germs of the old system survived the Islamic Revolution and carried on in influential positions within the State structures. Bani Sadr, the first President, and Sadiq Qutbzadeh, who briefly held the office of foreign minister and was later executed for conspiring to kill the Imam, are two of the best known examples of the 'liberals' who penetrated the system at its very heart. Both men were close to the Imam in Paris and had flown to Tehran with him. There were many others. Karim Sanjabi, Iran's first foreign minister after the Islamic Revolution, Ibrahim Yazdi, also foreign minister for a time, and Mehdi Bazargan, the first Prime Minister appointed by the Imam, are all examples of old germs surviving and prospering in the new climate. Clearly, too many of these germs had jumped on the revolutionary bandwagon and played havoc with it. Many of them were exposed and swiftly removed. This demonstrated the power and ability of the new order to detect hostile elements and to deal effectively with them.

At another level the new State kept the departmental structures of the old State, often in the same buildings, and most of its manpower. Hidden within the civil service were many opponents of the new Islamic order. Many of them had quickly grown beards and taken to offering prayers, at least during working hours. The havoc caused by these middle and lower ranks of the civil service is unknown and difficult to quantify. At the head of most departments were revolutionaries, with no experience of the workings of the system. Many of these revolutionaries, too, were young and grossly inexperienced in anything, let alone administration and decision-making. They had little guidance from the cabinet either because members of the cabinet were often as green as their juniors. The 'professionals' in the system made their new bosses look amateurs, if not downright idiotic. The size of the civil service was greatly swelled by political demands to give jobs to those who had made sacrifices for the new order. This increased the salary budget and reduced the efficiency of the system. Moving around the great offices of the State in Tehran one saw the damaging effects of this artificial increase in the size of the bureaucracy. The war and counter-revolutionary pressures meant the installation of new security systems. The new security apparatus sucked in a large number of young men who had been shouting slogans in the streets. They threw their considerable weight around and made the offices even less productive than they might otherwise have been. The security apparatus also had to import expensive four-wheel drive vehicles and highly sensitive electronic devices. Even junior ministers travelled in high security vehicles escorted by revolutionary guards. In time these became status symbols and it took years to get rid of them. The physical structure of these offices imposed their own value systems. For example, the size of the room was determined by the status of the official in the hierarchy, the room determined the size of his table, the table determined the size of the chair and the size of the conference table determined the size and numbers of chairs around it. Similar factors determined the number of telephones, the number of secretaries, cars, drivers and janitors on call. This physical environment ultimately determined the size of the man, especially his ego. Not one of them would fit into the example set by the Prophet, upon whom be peace, the Prophet's noble family or the *sahaba*. The élitist and hierarchical class structure of the late Pehlavi regime was fully repeated in the new Islamic regime. Holders of such high offices as President and Prime Minister, and a few others lower down the order, more than matched the simplicity and humility of Abu Bakr, Umar, Uthman and Ali. But the arrogance of many officials also matched and often exceeded the arrogance, flamboyance and ostentation of most rulers who followed the first four *khulafa*. This was so in Tehran and in the provinces. This was also the case in the embassies and other diplomatic missions around the world. Even in embassies there were some notable exceptions, but not many. The high standards set by Imam Khomeini, and followed by Ayatullah Sayyid Ali Khamenei after him, are thought to be fit only for a few people at the top. This ostentation was imposed by the structures of the *ancien regime*. The State structures could not take on board the modesty and simplicity that Islam requires of its public servants. On one occasion it was suggested to an ambassador that he should sell his 'residence' in the most expensive part of the capital city and move into a modest house in the suburbs. He was offended, and the unfortunate visitor was never invited again. Similarly, an oil painting of a nude hung in the residence of the Shah's former ambassador in a Western capital. The Islamic ambassador had it covered by a *chador*. He allowed visitors to peep behind it and took great delight at their embarrassment. Everyone who was close to the domestic and foreign bureaucracy of post-revolutionary Iran has many such stories to tell.

The structural continuity into post-revolutionary Iran is a subject that is certain to provoke many arguments in years to come. Some will argue that 'there was no choice' because the new rulers had to get their hands on 'the levers of power'. This argument assumes that power resided in the structures and to exercise power one had to get in the old driver's seat. This is the argument of one buying a secondhand car; not of a revolution setting up a new State and its structures. The old engine also swallowed and squandered enormous amounts of the resources of the State. Its primary role was to create and support a culture of dependency and loyalty to the regime. The system's salary structure and privileges were designed to achieve this purpose. If the bureaucracy actually performed some functions beneficial to the State or the people, this was incidental to their main purpose. This old engine was not suited to the ethos of the new Islamic State. There was evidence everywhere that the new Islamic operatives of the old machine enjoyed its plundering habits almost as much as their forerunners had done. The machine and its engine were enormously expensive to run. How this culture of waste and ostentation continued to thrive was reflected in the Foreign Ministry's insistence that Irani diplomats abroad must have chauffeur-driven black Mercedes limousines. Neither was the opulence of Iranian embassies, a legacy of the Shah's regime, cut back to any significant extent. Many new diplomats made great personal sacrifices. Some even slept in the basement of the embassy. In 1984, the whole of the 18-man Irani delegation to UNESCO in Geneva stayed in the basement of the embassy there. Their simple food and lifestyle, and prayers throughout the night, were indeed a moving experience. One Iranian ambassador passing through London took a bus from the airport to go and stay at a friend's house. But, sadly, such examples were few and far between. And everything cannot be blamed on the legacy of the Shah. For example, in capitals where new embassies had to be built and furnished, or rebuilt as in London, the level of opulence reached by the Shah's regime was repeated, even exceeded. But also hidden within this continuity of opulence was a rough notion of equality for the Islamic diplomats. They received a flat rate of modest pay whether they were posted at the UN in New York or in Sri Lanka. Thus the man in New York experienced great hardship while the man in Colombo accumulated huge savings. The point is that the highly stratified culture of the old élitist order also became a hiding place for many of doubtful revolutionary credentials. But equally there is no doubt that the truly committed revolutionaries among them were, and remain, men and women of great *taqwa* and piety. The fault, if it could be called that, lay in the revolutionary thought itself. It was naively assumed that the *taqwa* of the individual would overcome the arrogance that was a requirement of the system and its physical surroundings. Human nature being what it is, even an Eskimo living near the North Pole would, given a chance, begin to use a refrigerator.

The old order was also deeply nationalistic. It was as far removed from Islam as anything could be. Yet, for nearly three hundred years, the *usuli* movement had remained uncontaminated with Iranian nationalism. The *usuli* movement was born and bred entirely within the Shi'i tradition in Islam. In this respect also it was different from the Jama'at-e Islami of Mawlana Mawdoodi and Ikhwan al-Muslimoon of Hasan al-Banna. Mawdoodi and Banna felt that they had to take Pakistani and Arab nationalist sentiments on board their political thought and the Islamic parties they founded. The *usuli* ulama in Iran felt no such compulsion, though Ayatullah Kashani and others had been involved in the nationalist politics of Iran in the nineteen fifties. This was because the movement in Iran had been an open movement, open to all Muslims, and did not need the exclusivist structure of a political party. Because the movement was also an Islamic movement that did not want to fight and win elections, it did not need formal recognition or registration by the regime. It was a movement to overthrow the regime, not to defeat it at the polls. In the final months before the Islamic Revolution, it became the need of many nationalist parties and groups to join the movement and accept its leadership. The open movement approach gathers all on board, while the political party approach gets bogged down by early compromises and deals with existing political forces at work. Horse trading is inseparable from participation in the electoral process. In the end a great many nationalists joined the movement, hence the short periods in office enjoyed by such men as Bazargan, Sanjabi, Bani Sadr, Yazdi and

Qutbzadeh. But by then the Islamic Revolution had triumphed and the Imam was able to deal with this nuisance. However, a more sinister kind of nationalism was lurking in the State and administrative structures of the old order. This incipient nationalism has been in evidence in all of Iran's post-revolutionary attitudes at lower levels of government. Even the Constitution of the new Islamic State seemed to bestow a degree of respectability on Irani nationalism by providing, for instance, that the President of the State has to be racially Iranian. This Constitutional provision cannot be explained away by the decision, conscious or otherwise, to work through the former regime's State and administrative structures. This was a sop to nationalist elements present in the Revolutionary Council that drew up the Constitution.

Islamic Revolutions of the future must learn from Iran's experience. The triumph of the revolution must include the abolition of its State and administrative structures and the creation of an entirely new system of low cost domestic administration and modest diplomatic missions. Host countries do not care for the size, colour and make of the diplomat's car, or the size, furnishings and opulence of his house and embassy. Other States give due regard to diplomats, and even ordinary citizens, in relation to their country's domestic performance and efficiency in the management of their resouces. They assess a country by its power and influence, not by the size of the diplomat's car. If the ambassadors of the Islamic Republic of Iran walked on foot to present their credentials, they would carry more weight than, as at present, in big black Mercedes on which the Iranian Foreign Minister, Ali Akbar Vilayeti, is reported to have insisted. It is colonial, monarchical and democratic States that need the costly, top heavy, bureaucracy as a system of outdoor relief for its civil servants, supporters and the upper classes. Any State that sets out to serve the mass of its people and to create a just order has no option but to abolish the established and costly system of State structures and administration. Any government, Islamic or otherwise, that spends most of its income on itself, cannot also claim to be serving the people.

Curiously enough the leadership in Iran understood all this in the case of its universities and schools. The universities were closed down for three years. Teachers with secular orientations and their centres of power in the universities were systematically weeded out. New teachers with a commitment to the Islamic Revolution and the new Islamic State were brought in. Even the admission policies took the needs of the new State into account. In schools the syllabus and text books were thoroughly revised and all traces of the old culture removed. This is one of the greatest achievements of the Islamic Revolution and of the new leadership. It is therefore all the more surprising that similar action was not taken to rid all parts of the State's administrative structures of their wasteful habits. Even more damaging to the new Islamic State has been poor decision-making, although the public conduct of the high profile officials has been by and large exemplary. But at the level of provision of services and mass contact, the conduct of the civil servant has changed little. This leads many to complain that 'nothing has changed' or that 'it is still the same people'. This erodes the public standing of the Islamic Revolution and its leadership. It also allows Western writers to argue that 'political Islam is a failure' and that 'save for Iran, it has not won power in the States of the Muslim world...for all its incantation about an Islamic way, with a specific Islamic economy and Islamic State, the realities of the Muslim world remain fundamentally unchanged'[1]. A new partial revolution, or a series of partial or corrective revolutions, are required to supplement the grand victory of the Islamic Revolution of 1979. It would be wrong to regard the 1979 revolution as complete. Imam Khomeini himself regarded it as only the beginning of a long series of revolutionary measures that would follow[2].

It is also true that the leadership of the Islamic Revolution saw the need for new institutions to protect the fledgling Islamic State and to carry out some vital functions on its behalf. The best known among these was the Sepah-e Pasdaran-e Inqilab-e Islami, or the Revolutionary Guards. The Sepah, as it came to be known, was the leadership's own security apparatus. It proved highly effective against all domestic counter-revolutionary forces, including the violently Marxist Mujahideen-e Khalq Organisation (MKO) and also the liberal nationalist elements such as Bani Sadr and Qutbzadeh which had penetrated the new system. Imam Khomeini paid glowing tributes to the role of the Sepah saying 'there would be no revolution without the Sepah'. The second important organisation set up by the new leadership was the Jihad-e Sazindigi or Jihad for the Reconstruction of Life, or just Jihad for short. A group of highly motivated young graduate engineers, doctors, scientists and others joined the Jihad to develop the country's infrastructure, especially in housing and agriculture. Its organisation was simple and its method populist. A Jihad team would target a village and go there for a few weeks. They would live, eat, and sleep in the homes of the local people. Within weeks they would set up basic services such as clean piped water, improved hygiene, introduce modern agricultural and construction methods and then leave. They would leave behind no bureaucratic control or tell-tale stories of city dwellers having come and gone leaving the hapless villagers to meet high social costs of 'development'. They left behind them a grateful people who enjoyed a higher standard of living using existing local resources. There were no hidden social costs and their services cost the State exchequer nothing. The third important organisation to emerge during the war imposed by Iraq was the Baseej, or mobilisation. The Baseej consisted of young, lightly trained soldiers who had offered to fight alongside the professional army. The stories of their exploits and courage not only struck fear in the hearts of the Iraqi soldiers reading Playboy magazine in their bunkers, but also banished any thoughts of intervention that might have occurred to the two superpowers and their European and Arab allies. The great Islamic Revolution needs a series of smaller revolutions to take it on to new heights of motivation, mobilisation, voluntary service, power and achievement. The high and mighty in the Islamic State need to be seen to be humble and accessible. The costly and top-heavy structures of the ministries and ministers who occupy acres of office space and other resources are out of place in the Islamic State.

It is possible that the military campaigns of the Prophet Muhammad, upon whom be peace, were a form of deliberately-generated partial revolution to keep up the momentum and build upon the power and ascendancy that was achieved through *hijra,* or migration to Medina. It is also possible that Ba'athist Iraq's war on Iran helped to consolidate the authority of the Islamic Revolution and its leadership. If the war was a western attempt to probe the defences of revolutionary Iran, or to soften up Iran with a view to a more direct Western military intervention at a later date, then the adventure failed. The war in fact hardened up Iran and made it impossible for the West to contemplate direct military action against the Islamic State. By successfully fighting this war over eight years, Iran may well have saved itself from a more demanding and damaging war in the future. The ulama of Iran went to the battlefield with the troops and nearly one thousand of them were martyred. This gave the ulama's leadership a great deal more credibility than the mere holding or competing for political office in Tehran might have done. In the war Iran lost many of its youth and physical resources. But a new State must fight and win a war early in its life to ensure its long-term survival. It was good to show all those who might have been tempted what they would be taking on if they were to invade Islamic Iran. It was Iran's performance in its own Gulf war that ultimately saved it from involvement in the West's 1991 Gulf expedition to 'liberate' its own colony, Kuwait, from the ambitions of its other local client, Saddam Hussain. A successful war is a good investment in the future. Anyone who gets defeated in a war has to fight another war and win in order to survive in the long term. If this is not possible, as Germany and Japan found after 1945, then they have to achieve an 'economic miracle' that has left the victors wondering who won the war after all. Germany and Japan have developed an alternative source of power. With this power most of the gains that the victorious allies made have been cancelled. Germany now dominates Europe as it always wanted to, and Japan dominates the Far East. The gains they have made through economic dominance cannot be cancelled by military means. The strength of their respective currencies is playing havoc with the once almighty US dollar and pound sterling. Germany and Japan could hardly have done better had they won the war. Ultimately it is the factors of internal cohesion and the quality of leadership and government that determines the outcome of a long-term struggle for at least some control over one's immediate environment. The greater the internal cohesion and output of economic and other resources the more chance a State has of exercising some control or influence over at least parts of the world system.

It is here that the challenge of Islam is specific. Islam claims that it is the best means of internal cohesion among a people and the best means of cooperation and peace among all peoples. It does not claim to eliminate war, but it claims that if blood must be spilled this should not be for territorial or economic gain, but for a higher moral purpose that shall benefit all mankind. Islam also claims to produce the highest quality leadership and government. These claims of Islam were converted into historical facts in the golden era of Islam - in the lifetime of the Prophet, upon whom be peace, and in the period of the first four *rashidoon,* or rightly guided, caliphs. The Islamic Revolution must inaugurate a system of leadership, government and obedience to them by the people that takes up the threads of history broken off by the Umaiyyads. The Islamic Revolution must also define the 'good society' and show the way to its achievement. The Islamic Revolution is not simply the overthrowal of an autocratic ruler and his corrupt entourage, and the installation of a new leadership in power.

This leads us to attempt a layman's operational definition of an Islamic State. The Islamic State is a State in which the leadership, the government and the people have a single defined purpose. This can only happen if the leadership is clearly and demonstrably *muttaqi,* and if the *ba'ya* or obedience given by the populace is also equally clearly and demonstrably based on *taqwa. Taqwa,* or piety, holds and binds the political system of Islam together. The system then dispenses *'adl* (justice) to all. It is the *taqwa* of all its componant parts and their combined output, *'adl,* that legitimise the Islamic State.

Taqwa and *'adl,* therefore, are crucial concepts. Let us deal with *taqwa* first and develop a wider and deeper understanding of it than the usual 'Godfearing' variety. To begin with let us look at the range of meanings in a dictionary, beginning with its Arabic roots *waqa (waqy, wiqaya)* - to guard, preserve something, take good care of; to safeguard, shield, shelter, preserve, protect, keep something from, guard something against; to protect, offer or afford protection against; to prevent, obviate a danger. *ittaqa* - to beware, be wary of, guard, to be on one's guard, protect something, make sure against, to fear God. *waqi* - protection, safeguard. *waqa', wiqa'* - protection, prevention. *wiqaya* - protection, prevention, precaution, obviation, averting; defence against. *wiqqaya* - protective covering. *wiqa'i* - preventive, as in preventive medicine *(tibb). waqiy* - protecting; protector, preserver, guardian. *taqwa* - devoutness, piety. *tuqan* - godliness, devoutness, piety. *taqiy* - godfearing, godly, devout, pious. *taqiya* - fear, caution, prudence...

The dictionary goes on a bit, but we have taken sufficient to liberate *taqwa* from its narrow confines. The dictionary meaning of *'adl* and its various derivatives is also equally wide-ranging. We must give them broader and political dimensions. As the two all-inclusive attributes that legitimise the origin and conduct of the component parts of the Islamic State, and the Islamic State as a whole, perhaps a separate book-length study would be required to deal with these key concepts and their many dimensions. All that we need to note here is that the Islamic State, therefore, is not a totalitarian, liberal or democratic Leviathan put together to pursue the narrowly defined 'national', class, ethnic or colonial/imperialist interests of its leadership, government or people. The Islamic State is a moral structure with equal responsibilities towards all mankind. The Islamic State is put together by those who are committed to order their individual and collective lives according to a moral paradigm defined by Allah *(subhanahu wa ta'ala)*. The moral, behavioural and historical validity of the paradigm is provided by the Qur'an and the *Sirah* and *Sunnah* of the Prophet, upon whom be peace.

NOTES:

1. See, for example, Olivier Roy, *The Failure of Political Islam,* London:I.B. Tauris & Co, 1994.

2. Speeches and declarations of Imam Khomeini, in Ruhullah Khomeini, *Islam and Revolution,* Berkeley: The Mizan Press, 1981.

Chapter 8

Convergence at the core: *khilafah/imamah*

Islam is all about leadership. Leadership, and the power of the Leader, are central to Islam. Let us, in the style of Islam's first doctrine - there is no god but Allah - first look at the kind of leadership or rulership Islam does not recognise as legitimate. A leader who conquers land and people, and sets himself up as its ruler or king, has no legitimacy and must be fought against. Similar is the position with regard to other rulers, or institutions of government such as parliaments, political parties, councils, regimes, juntas, and even 'elected representatives'. They must be fought against and overthrown as soon as possible. Obedience to such rulers, or authorities, is allowed under conditions of unbearable duress, but only as a temporary expedience until such time as they can be overthrown.

Let us digress and consider a metaphor. Imagine a country that has a single powerhouse supplying power to the national grid, and through it to all households, offices, shops, industries, schools, universities, hospitals, roads, railways, airlines and all other functional systems. In such a situation all appliances using power would have to have a standard plug that must be inserted into the socket before power will flow into them. All of them have to be compatible with one another. Islam, too, is such an integrated, all-inclusive system of power, authority and obedience. In Islam the powerhouse, or the source of all power, is Allah *(subhanahu wa ta'ala)* Alone. This is the doctrine of *tawhid,* or absolute Oneness of Allah Who has no partners. Every*thing* and every*one* must submit to the power of Allah[1]. Every*thing*, including animals, are programmed by the Creator to obey Him. The choice of disobedience has not been given to them. Only *man* ('man' here includes women) has been given the choice of obedience and/or disobedience. Those among men and women who choose to obey Allah are called Muslims, or those who submit[2].

Next we must understand the role of Muhammad, upon whom be peace, in the power grid of Islam. In this grid the Prophet is the only direct human link with Allah. He received the Message and became its last and sole Exemplar[3]. The line of obedience is clearly defined. Obey Allah, obey Allah's Prophet and he from among you [the obedient ones] who is in charge of the affairs [of the community][4]. It is this second human link, after the Prophet, that completes the circuit of the flow of Divine power to the human condition who is called *khalifah* or *imam,* or, more precisely, *khalifatur Rasool.* In this study these terms are used interchangeably. The processes of the convergence of the two terms as they have developed in Shi'i and Sunni schools of thought will be discussed presently.

Let us first examine the dictionary meaning of the root *khalafa*: to be the successor of someone, succeed someone; to follow someone; to take the place of someone, to substitute for someone; to replace someone or something; to stay behind after someone's departure; to appoint as successor to someone...

In this power grid of Islam, Allah and the Prophet are constants. Those who follow the Prophet change from time to time. Once the successor, *khalifah*, to the Prophet is in place, obedience to the *khalifah* and his 'government' or, to those he may appoint in positions of authority, is obedience to Allah and His Prophet and therefore obligatory on all Muslims. The *khalifah* must conduct the affairs of the Islamic State by *shura*[5]. For this purpose the *khalifah* may create, again through *shura*, a consultative system based on a *majlis as-shura*, personal advisers, president, prime minister, cabinet, ministries to administer offices of State on his behalf, provincial and district governors and lower level officials. In fact the entire structure of the Islamic State, down to its most junior or minor operative, is an extension of the authority of the *khalifah/imam* whose authority, in turn, is derived from the authority of Allah and His Prophet.

Following the metaphor of the single powerhouse and an all-inclusive grid of power, the *khalifah* is the single human link that connects the Ummah to the power and authority of Allah and His Prophet. It is the presence of the *khilafah* of the Prophet that legitimises the power and authority of the political system. If there is no *khalifah,* there is no *khilafah* and therefore no power or authority. Indeed, there can be no Islamic State unless it is a *khilafah* ruled over by a single ruler who is *khalifatur Rasool* (successor to the Prophet). On this issue, contrary to popular belief, there is no dispute between Sunni and Shi'i positions. As Abul-Fazl Ezzati puts it, in Shi'i terminology, *imamat* means 'absolute divine leadership' of the Muslim community in all religious and secular affairs of the *imams* [of the *ahl al-bait]* who, in succession to the Prophet, lead the community as the viceregents of Allah, for mankind is the viceregent of Allah. The authority of *imam,* however, is not direct, independent authority but he enjoys this authority as the successor *[khalifah]* of the Prophet'. Ezzati adds: 'But in the absence of the Prophet and *imam,* both the Sunnis and the Shi'i believe that the Muslim community has the divine right to choose their own leader'[6].

The political structure of Islam begins to take shape after the Leader is in place. The Leader is the central point of the structure. The structure is built around him. He is the 'plug', the essential link, the conduit or the intermediary who draws power and legitimacy from the ultimate source. Power can only flow along channels that are compatible with the leader's own source of power, which is of course Allah *(subhanahu wa ta'ala).* This power can only be used for goals and purposes that are also compatible with the Divine purpose. Change is endemic in the human condition, as we noted at the beginning of this study. The Leader's duty is to manage, direct, guide, influence, anticipate, manipulate and control change while keeping firm to the Divine foundations of belief, knowledge, morality and piety. Most issues affecting the life of the community are subject to choice and involve decision-making. Each decision or choice, however private or public, must be guided by the bounds of *taqwa.* In Islam the collective or public good always has a higher value than personal, private or small group interest.

It is in the area of choice and decision-making that the political process must operate. In secular societies that also claim to be 'democratic' there is a constant struggle to change the moral foundations of the society. In Britain, for example, within the last 40 years the country's 'sovereign' parliament has legalised such things as homosexuality, abortion and gambling. Prostitution was never illegal. The 'sovereign' parliament has also abolished the death penalty. In an Islamic State, or *khilafah*, such issues have been decided by Divine revelation and the *Sirah* and the *Sunnah* of the Prophet, upon whom be peace, for all time to come. No amount of 'scientific' research or weight of contrived 'public opinion' can change these moral parameters. Nor can public opinion, parliament, political parties, or 'scientific research' change the position, power and role of the *khalifah*. The *khalifah,* because he is closest to Allah *(subhanahu wa ta'ala)* and His Prophet and is the living manifestation of the Prophet's power and authority, cannot be overruled. However, the *khalifah,* in the light of advice given to him and the weight of public opinion, may change his mind. But if the *khalifah* decides not to change his mind, obedience to him is obligatory.

In matters of decision-making and choice, it is part of the *khalifah's* Divine duty to ensure that widest possible recourse to consultation is made available. Public opinion can form part of consultation, provided public opinion is made through information and education and not through propaganda of vested interests represented by political parties, the media, advertising and professional lobbies. It is possible, for instance, that a future *khalifah* may make use of the country's universities as centres of research on the basis of which the State may make its decisions. Universities, other seats of learning and specialist bodies, may also propose new legislation or changes in the law. They may also review and evaluate current policies and propose changes or put forward options for entirely new policies.

The Islamic State can function on the basis of developing centres of excellence and does not need political parties. The *majlis as-shura* (the parliament) may be composed of individuals chosen or elected, or a mixture of both, on the basis of their standing and reputation in their localities, towns or cities. In the working of the *majlis, ad hoc* groups may emerge on specific issues and dissolve themselves when those issues have been resolved. In this way the *khalifah* himself, a department of State or a university or any other body proposing legislation will have to convince a majority of the members of the *majlis* in open debate. There will be no 'party whip' or secret deals, horse trading and arm twisting to secure majorities as is the case in secular 'democracies'. Decision and legislation in the Islamic State will be in pursuit of the moral and just society as defined by Islam rather than in pursuit of the 'greatest good of the greatest number' and other similar ideas that are the foundations of secular liberal democracies. Moral correctness of all its people individually and all individuals together is the highest good to be pursued by the State and all its functionaries.

Moral correctness is not merely a reference to such matters as marriage, divorce and inheritance; moral correctness includes the economic structure of society and the regulation of disparities of bargaining power arising out of unequal positions in exchange relationships. The Prophet of Islam, upon whom be peace, established a mosque in Medina which has been rebuilt and extended many times down the centuries. But the Prophet also established a market and regulated it. That market and its regulatory rules have been forgotten. Traces of it are found in sources now almost entirely inaccessible. There is no mention of them in the modern literature on the *Sirah* and the *Sunnah*. The legitimising of modern crude capitalism as 'Islamic' is a gross distortion of Islam. Neither is Islam a godly form of communism or socialism.

Many contemporary readers, brought up on the literature put out by Jama'at-e Islami and Ikhwan al-Muslimoon, will be startled by the statement that Islam in fact does not have an 'economic system' as such. Any economic system that is created and regulated by the Islamic State to secure a just and equitable return for all factors of production, exchange and distribution is acceptable. Obviously the Islamic State would not tolerate gross inequalities in income and levels of consumption in a Muslim society because to do so would contradict the principle of *'adl,* or justice. For the same reason, all traces of exploitation, low income, excessive profits, ostentatious consumption, poverty and need have to be eradicated. The transfer of income, savings, investment and other resources from surplus to deficient areas will have to be made. Income from natural and mineral resources will have to be equitably shared. It is possible that the optimum level of happiness and justice for all is secured at a lower level of output and consumption rather than at the highest level of output and consumption. If so, then the lower level of output and consumption may be preferred by public policy than the higher level until conditions become suitable for growth. The rearranging of old furniture, or even throwing a few pieces away, often yields higher satisfaction than adding more to the stock. More consumption can yield less satisfaction, as is evident in Western societies where the rate of suicides among the well off is higher than among the poor. As standards of living and standards of medical care of the elderly are rising in the West, also rising are demands for legalised euthanasia. More and more people do not wish to live out the natural term of their lives. Even their families and relatives often want to be rid of the elderly. The assumption that more means better and happier is untenable. The policies of the Islamic State in matters of housing and the distribution and utilisation of land, mineral, water and other resources will be similarly affected by moral parameters.

The *khalifah/imam* and his *khilafah* (the Islamic State) are Divine instruments for the maximisation of good and the minimisation of evil in the human condition in all parts of the world. This is also a primary consideration in foreign policy and in decisions affecting war and peace.

The crucial question that remains to be considered is: how does the Leader emerge in the absence of the Islamic State? Once the Islamic State is in place we can assume that a mechanism will also exist to choose or appoint the *khalifah's* successor. Our primary concern now is the emergence of leadership of the Islamic movement leading up to the establishment of the Islamic State. As has already been noted, the political structure of Islam begins to take shape after the Leader is in place. The Leader is the central point of the structure. The structure is built around him. The structure begins with him and he is its supreme architect. The question that then arises is how does the Leader emerge?

The point to note is that there is never a total absence of leadership in the Muslim community. In the absence of the supreme Leader, the *khalifatur Rasool*, at the head of the community, leadership roles continue to exist at lower levels of the community. For example, the husband and father in the household is also the leader of the household and his authority in matters affecting the family is as total as the authority of the *khalifah* in his *khilafah*. Similar is the authority of the *imam* during prayer. If the *imam* makes a mistake those behind him may indicate to the *imam* that he has made a mistake, but if the *imam* does not correct himself then those behind must follow him in his error. The condition of obedience to lower levels of leadership in society is the *taqwa* of the persons concerned. This is why many *sufi* shaikhs command almost Divine authority over their followers. Indeed, *sufi* orders invariably view themselves as non-territorial Islamic States. Some leaders of *sufi* orders have gone on to try to establish the *khilafah* and have engaged in *jihad* towards this goal. Othman dan Fodio, who established the Sokoto *khilafah* in West Africa in 1810, and the *jihad* movement of Sayyid Ahmed Shahid (d.1831) of India, immediately come to mind. There have been many others.

There are three examples we need to examine closely. They are Hasan al-Banna, Maulana Mawdoodi and Imam Khomeini. All three were born within a few years of each other at the beginning of the twentieth century. Banna was assassinated by King Farouq's British-run secret service in 1949 when in his forties. Mawdoodi died in 1979 and Imam Khomeini in 1989. All three in their own ways set out to establish the *khilafah*. Banna and Mawdoodi became great leaders of 'Islamic parties' that tried to establish 'Islamic States' on the foundations of nationalism and post-colonial nation-States. Even this limited goal their 'Islamic parties' have not achieved. Imam Khomeini alone succeeded in establishing the Islamic State, became its supreme Leader taking the title of *vali-e faqih*. According to one version communicated to the author by more than one source, Imam Khomeini did not take the title of *khalifah* or *khalifatur Rasool* or *imam* because, in his view, neither Shi'i nor Sunni Muslims were ready to accept him in that role. He had to find an intermediary title for his position in Iran. He may also have been aware of the fact that he had come from the tradition of *marjaiyyat* and many *maraje'* senior to him in rank were then living in Iran and Iraq. The title he chose for himself was *vali-e faqih,* but within months he became known, by popular acclaim, as the *Imam,* or the Leader. 'Imam' is a term also used by Sunni Muslims as interchangeable with *khalifah*.

The difference between Imam Khomeini, Banna and Mawdoodi is that Imam Khomeini emerged as the embodiment of an intellectual tradition begun among the ulama and the religious establishment in the Shi'i school some two hundred years before, while Banna and Mawdoodi devised and generated their own political ideas and party structures. There had been no experience or tradition of political parties in the history of Islam. Banna's and Mawdoodi's parties, their structures and political roles were, consciously or unconsciously, modelled on the political parties of Europe or of similar parties started by the colonial elites in India and Egypt. Banna's and Mawdoodi's attempts were elementary and tentative with little or no depth in history, theology or intellectual tradition. Their ideas did not become accepted as dominant Muslim political thought even in the nation-States that they chose as their immediate target areas. In the context of Sunni political thought, badly bruised through its association with *mulukiyyah,* Banna's and Mawdoodi's attempts were not likely to be more than exploratory first attempts. Their long-term contribution is likely to be limited to the elimination of the party political structure and the democratic method as realistic options for the global Islamic movement or any part of it. They should go down in history as the first explorers who started off on the long uncharted road to recovery after a nightmare period in Muslim history. The fact that they or their parties did not get very far down the road, or up the mountain, is not their fault. But the fact also is that had it not been for their contributions, the movement in Iran might have made the same mistakes as they did. The future of the global Islamic movement will be the richer for their contribution.

Throughout this study reference has been made to an ongoing process of convergence of the various strains of Muslim political thought. This convergence has to be part of an intellectual revolution. The outlines of this intellectual revolution are already in place and have been identified in the earlier chapters. This process of convergence must begin at the core of the political structures of Islam. This core, clearly, is the leadership. It was on this issue that the earliest difference of opinion occurred. Yet the position of the Leader *(khalifah/imam)* in Islam is the simplest and most clearly defined and easily understood concept. There is no ambiguity on this issue. The differences have revolved around the issues of who and how, not whether or not there should be a Leader. On the issues of the Leader's source of authority and his right to obedience there has been no dispute.

The issue of who and how, in a sense predates Islam. Religious communities in those days, chiefly Jews and Christians, knew from their scriptures that another Prophet would come. But they wanted the Prophet to be from among them. Bahira, a Christian monk living in Busra in the area of Ash-Sham, told the Prophet's uncle Abu Talib, that he saw signs of future prophethood in Muhammad who was then only 12. Bahira advised Abu Talib not to take Muhammad too far into Ash-Sham for fear lest the Jews, too, recognised the signs of future prophethood in Muhammad. Bahira feared that the Jews might harm Muhammad because he was not from among them. Many years later in Makkah, another Christian monk, Waraqa bin Nawfal, a cousin of the Prophet's wife Khadijah, also recognised the signs of impending prophethood in Muhammad and delivered a similar warning. Bahira and Waraqa, living far apart, shared a sense of history derived from their scriptures and this told them that another great prophet was about to come. Each recognised that the conditions of *jahiliyyah* (ignorance and moral depravity) that prevailed then required the advent of a prophet. There had been prophets throughout history, so they waited for another. But they were also aware that the peoples of the time would have wanted him to be from among themselves. A similar situation arose in Medina at the death of the Prophet Muhammad, upon whom be peace. All Muslims agreed that the prophethood had ended for all time and that there should be a *khalifatur Rasool* to carry on the duties of the head of the Islamic State.

It is beyond the scope of this study to trace the course of increasing divergence that occurred in the Shi'i and Sunni positions on the issues of who and how. Suffice to say that secondary or man-made theology written on both sides to define their respective positions made the situation even worse than it need have been. A complicating factor, among the Sunnis from the beginning of Umaiyyad rule, and among the Shi'is during the Safavid period in Iran, was the pressure on their respective theologians to meet the dynastic needs of the rulers. Earlier, once *malukiyyah* had become established as the norm and legitimised in Sunni thought, the Shi'i ulama took up the extreme position that no legitimate Islamic State could be established until the coming of Imam Mehdi *(alayhis salaam)*. This position was known as *akhbari* in which the Shi'i ulama's only role was to compile and communicate the *hadith* of the Prophet, upon whom be peace, and the explanation of *hadith* as made by the *imams* of the Prophet's pure and noble family. This amounted to suspending the office of the *khalifah* until the coming of Imam Mehdi. It virtually forbade the Shi'i from participation in the political life of the Ummah. It is difficult to say whose divergence was worse or greater - the Sunni acceptance of *mulukiyyah* and other forms of government as worthy of obedience, or the *akhbari* position among the Shi'i that suspended all political manifestations of Islam altogether. The net result of both the Sunni and Shi'i positions was the same: the eventual dismemberment of the Ummah and defeat and occupation by foreign powers.

Here one must pause to note that the Prophet, upon whom be peace, brought only one Islam. The two, Sunni and Shi'i, and other versions of Islam, are the result of historical forces that led to divergences in *ijtihad* (independent legal judgement on issues not settled in the Qur'an and *Sunnah*). Muhammad, upon whom be peace, was the last prophet and Islam the complete message. As such Islam must include within it the dynamism, versatility, and feedback learning processes capable of correcting the divergences. The area of choice given to mankind includes the possibility of divergence. But it also includes the mechanism of *ijtihad* which allows for learning from the results of choices made in the past. In the early phase of history the ulama of the Shi'i and Sunni schools made a great deal of *ijtihad*. Having legitimised their respective divergences they then closed the doors of *ijtihad*. Having locked themselves in and thrown away the keys of *ijtihad,* both sets of ulama could do little more than write more 'theology' in defence of their earlier divergences. This compounded their deviation as succeeding generations and new rulers added to the confusion.

In this situation it was inevitable that their respective untenable positions would lead to great damage to Muslims and the political structures and power of Islam in the world. And it did. The results of accumulated failures and their unbearable costs over hundreds of years were bound to force revision and reassessment of untenable positions.

And this was bound to reopen the doors of *ijtihad*. It was also inevitable that whichever school in Islam, Shi'i or Sunni, was the first to reopen the doors of *ijtihad* would generate the intellectual revolution that is a precursor to the Islamic Revolution and the setting up of the Islamic State. It so happened that the debate within the Shi'i school challenging the *akhbari* position was the first to mature into a new school of thought among Shi'i ulama.

Such ulama became known as the *usulioon* or those who engaged in *ijtihad* based on the *usul*, or basic principles of Islam. This is known in Shi'i history as the *'usuli* revolution'. Gradually the *akhbari* ulama gave way to the *usulioon*. But, in the tradition of all revolutions, there are at first many partial revolutions. The most important outcome of this early partial revolution in the Shi'i school, emerging from the *usuli* re-examination, was *marjaiyyat* as a form of interim leadership until the coming of Imam Mehdi *(alayhis salaam)*. Every Shi'i Muslim had to be the *muqallid* (follower) of a *marja'* *(pl. maraje')*. This created a hierarchy among the Shi'i ulama. For all practical purposes each *marja'* performed the role of the *khalifah* for his followers. They did not command rulership over territory, but they ruled over the religious behaviour of vast numbers of people. Gradually some *maraje'* became very powerful, able to challenge the secular authority of the Shah. The first great clash between the authority of the leading *marja'* of the time and Qajar dynasty occurred in 1892 over the grant of the tobacco monopoly to the British. The monopoly collapsed when Ayatullah Mirza Hasan Shirazi issued a *fatwa* to the effect that so long as tobacco in Iran was distributed by the British its consumption was *haram* (forbidden). Subsequent partial revolutions leading up to the total Islamic Revolution of 1979 have been dealt with in chapter five. The point to note here is that once a single step in the right direction is taken, the dynamism of Islam is such that it guides those seeking to recover from error and deviation to all subsequent steps and stages in that direction. Nothing happens overnight.

The passage of time and the step by step accumulation of experience and results are the essence of the method of Islam. This happens in all directions. One error leads to another; deviance becomes a self-perpetuating habit; attempts to correct the error takes time, but once a bold step has been taken through an intellectual

102

revolution, Islam guides the faithful back to the correction of the initial error and convergence with itself. Many generations, indeed many centuries, may pass between the initial error and the final correction of error and convergence.

Thus, in the Shi'i tradition, once the *usulioon* of the 18th century had started the process of correction and convergence, it was only a matter of time that someone of the stature of Imam Khomeini would emerge and complete the process. But the rapidly expanding *usuli* establishment suffered from two weaknesses. The first was the senior ulama's self-imposed abstinence from seeking ultimate political power, and second was the multiplicity of *maraje'*. At any one time, a number of Grand Ayatullahs claimed large followings and often competed for followers *(muqallidin)*. These two handicaps are closely linked. So long as the ulama did not contemplate the exercise of supreme political power there was no need for a single leader, and so long as there was no single leader, a kind of *marja'* of *maraje'*, the exercise of ultimate political authority in the style of a *khalifah* could not be contemplated. Imam Ruhullah Khomeini did not claim to be *khalifah*, because in his judgement, the Ummah was not ready to accept him in that role. Perhaps another inhibiting factor was that there then lived many *maraje'* who were senior to him both in age and in the Shi'i hierarchy. A head of State taking the title of *khalifah* would have to override the authority of all other *maraje'*. This might have been too much even for the *usulioon* at that stage. Already through the Islamic Revolution Imam Khomeini had transformed Shi'i theology in some very important respects. It was clearly against prudence to alienate the citadels of power within the Shi'i tradition. In any such situation, even a revolution, it is important not to open all flanks at once. So Imam Khomeini took the title of *vali-e faqih*. Ayatullah Amid Zanjani, a constitutional expert in Iran, told the author that the term *vali-e faqih* was first used in Imam Ghazali's celebrated book, *Ahiyya-e Uloom*, written in the sixth century of the Hijri calendar. Imam Ghazali had argued that there should be an official called *vali-e faqih* to oversee the decisions of the *sultan* of the time. Imam Khomeini now used the term as an euphemism for *khalifah*. Imam Khomeini waited for almost 10 years before making it clear that he, as *vali-e faqih*, exercised all the authority available to the *khalifah*. In a *fatwa* issued on January 6, 1988, Imam Khomeini said that the Islamic government represents 'absolute sovereign power as delegated by Allah *(subhanahu wa ta'ala)* to the Prophet, upon whom be peace.' This, said Imam Khomeini, 'is the most important of Divine precepts *(ahkam)* and takes precedence over all the other secondary Divine precepts.' Imam Khomeini added: 'If the powers of Islamic government are to be confined within the framework of secondary Divine precepts, then the form of Divine rule and absolute sovereignty as delegated to the Prophet, upon whom be peace, would be a senseless and hollow phenomenon.' If this were so, he added, the legislative and administrative powers of Islamic government would be severely restricted. Imam Khomeini went on to give many examples of legislative, administrative, military and economic policies that would be impossible to implement if the Islamic government was bound by secondary Divine precepts. These include the acquisition by the State of private property for major public works, e.g., new roads, compulsory military service, regulation of foreign trade, prohibition of hoarding, customs and excise, taxation and fair pricing of goods and services. Imam Khomeini then argued that Islamic government 'which is part of the absolute sovereign power of Allah's Prophet, upon whom be peace, is one of the primary precepts of Islam and take precedence over all the secondary precepts.'

The position that the political power exercised by the Prophet must be inherited in full by the rulers who follow him has always been clear in Sunni thought. This is exactly how the four *rashidoon khulafah* (rightly guided caliphs) understood the source of their authority. The Islamic government is only an extension of the authority of the Leader, who is a *khalifah* (vicegerent) of the Prophet. This *fatwa* from Imam Khomeini has completed the long process of correction within the Shi'i school that had been at the very heart of the *usuli* intellectual revolution that began more than 200 years ago. The present Constitution of the Islamic State of Iran is a man-made document and has its faults, especially the provision that the President has to be of Iranian origin. But all the provisions in the matter of the appointment of the Leader, the *vali-e faqih,* whom we now know to be *khalifatur Rasool,* vicegerent of the Prophet, are fully compatible with the classical Sunni position on this vital issue.

After this convergence, for all practical purposes, on issues of Leadership, State and politics there is no longer any difference between the Sunni and Shi'i positions. Despite this, ulama on both sides are reluctant to openly acknowledge that this is so; they have to protect the vast amounts of deviant theological tracts that their elders have written over hundreds of years. On the Shi'i side, their religious structures and institutions are entirely based on sectarianism. They fear the collapse of these structures. But my initial paper on this subject, *Processes of error, deviation, correction and convergence in Muslim political thought*, published in 1989, has been translated into Arabic and Farsi and published in mass circulation newspapers and academic journals in Iran[7]. It is also generally known among the ulama in Iran that the Leader, Ayatullah al-Uzma Sayyid Ali Khamenei, accepts the arguments presented in the paper as valid. On the Sunni side the paper is as yet little known. But those who know of it have tried not to notice it. They, too, suffer from the disabilities imposed by the structures of their religious institutions and, more importantly in their case, by their 'religious' political parties. Some of them, such as the Jama'at/Ikhwan duopoly, fear the loss of their Saudi links. They fear that a new intellectual revolution would unite the Ummah over their heads.

This is where the role of the global Islamic movement is vital. It has already been argued that the global Islamic movement also has to act as an Open University of Islam. In this role the Islamic movement cannot become a 'party' in the Ummah. The Islamic movement must not have boundaries and frontiers and membership. It has to carry everyone, including the Jama'at/Ikhwan duopoly, within its fold. The Islamic movement must be an open system in every respect - structurally, intellectually and spiritually. This was the method of Prophet Muhammad, upon whom be peace. Even today this method is the most suited to overcome the global challenges that face Islam.

NOTES:

1. Al-Qur'an 3:17,79; 5:5; 6:125; 39:23; 61:17.

2. Ibid. 22:77; 33:35; 49:14.

3. Ibid. 33:21.

4. Ibid. 4:59.

5. Ibid. 42:38.

6. Abul-Fazl Ezzati, *'The Concept of Leadership in Islam'*, London: The Muslim Institute, Seminar Paper No 15, 1979.

7. This paper is included as an appendix in this volume.

Appendix*

Processes of error, deviation, correction and convergence in Muslim political thought

Bahira was a Christian monk living in Busra. Abu Talib, the Prophet's uncle, had taken Muhammad, then 12 years old, to Ash-Sham with a trading caravan. There Bahira recognised the signs of future prophethood in Muhammad, as told in Christian sources. Bahira advised the Prophet's uncle not to take Muhammad too far into Ash-Sham, for fear that the Jews might recognise the signs and try to harm the boy. Many years later in Makkah, another Christian, Waraqa bin Nawfal, a cousin of the Prophet's wife Khadija, also recognised the signs of impending prophethood in Muhammad's early experiences in the cave of Hira, and delivered a similar warning.

Neither Bahira nor Waraqa *knew* that Muhammad was the promised prophet, but both shared a sense of history derived from their religion, Christianity. They knew that a prophet would come; they did not know when or where or who he might be. Each recognised the condition of *jahiliyyah* that prevailed in their time required the coming of a prophet. Bahira and Waraqa were relying on Christian sources that were, even in their time, unreliable. Today, 14 centuries after the completion of the Qur'an, the final message of Allah, about which there is no doubt, and after the coming of the last Prophet, it should be easier to recognise signs foreshadowing current and future events.

How accurately we can do so depends on our understanding of the Islamic framework of history. For example, we do not know when Allah *subhanahu wa ta'ala* created the first man, Adam, who was

This paper was written in 1988-89. The understanding of the processes of historical change developed in it forms the basis of the analysis presented in this volume.

also a prophet. But what we do know is that between Adam, the first Prophet, and Muhammad, the last Prophet, there were perhaps as many as 124,000 other prophets, may Allah's peace and blessings be upon them all. The point is that Allah *subhanahu wa ta'ala* clearly took great care and a very long time preparing the world for the coming of the last Prophet and for the completion of His message to mankind. All this cannot have been for a matter of about 1400 years or thereabouts before the end of the world.

The view of history that we Muslims must take is that of course the end of the world will come, but its timing is known to Allah *subhanahu wa ta'ala* alone. He has not shared this knowledge with anyone, not even the prophets. It is, therefore, idle to speculate about it. In the meantime we must remember that, 1400 years after the completion of prophethood and revelation, Islam has yet to create a world in the image of itself, according to the Creator's own prescription for the world and everything in it. Perhaps a more realistic view is that though Islam as a message and a model was completed 1400 years ago, the main business of history, that is, bringing all mankind to Islam, is incomplete.

This raises another question: if the very long time before the completion of Islam was merely a 'preparatory period', how do we explain the last 1400 years? The *jahiliyyah* before Islam was perhaps an insufficient experience for man to realise the consequences of deviating from Islam. It may be useful to view these 1400 years as a practical demonstration of what happens to mankind, especially Muslims, when they deviate from the *sirat al-mustaqim*. This could only be demonstrated *after* Islam had been completed, not before. Perhaps the neo-*jahiliyyah* that prevails in the world today is just such a demonstration.

The deviation from Islam is of two sorts. There are those who never entered Islam, chose to fight it, and built for themselves a civilization and culture of *kufr* and *jahiliyyah*. Today this civilisation of *kufr* and *jahiliyyah* is represented by the western civilisation. This civilisation is global and includes many non-western sub-cultures, such as the Chinese, Japanese and Indian sub-cultures. It also includes some residual religious traditions, for example, post-Renaissance

Christianity, zionist-Judaism and militant Hinduism, all of which insist upon repudiating and rejecting Islam. Lastly, the western civilisation also includes those Muslims who have, under the influence of colonial domination, accepted the validity of secularism as a way of life. These Muslims represent all the ruling classes in Muslim societies today, except in post-Revolutionary Iran. The second type of deviation is within Islam. Such deviation is spearheaded by those *ulama*, of all schools of thought, who, for whatever reason, have accepted and legitimised political, social, cultural and other systems that do not conform with the Qur'an and the *Sunnah* of the Prophet, upon whom be peace. Examples of such deviation, including deviant theology, can be found everywhere.

However, deviation within Islam is mostly error that has accumulated with the passage of time. Such error is relatively easy to correct because the overall framework of Islam that binds the *Ummah* has not been breached.[1] The corrective power of Islam is represented by the inherent *taqwa* of even those who have erred. There have always existed *ulama*, of all schools of thought, who were willing and able to eliminate error and to bind the *Ummah* together.

The number of the so-called *ulama* committed to *fitna* and permanent divisions in the *Ummah* has always been small, though vocal because they have also enjoyed the political patronage of rulers bent upon transforming error into long-term, even permanent, deviation. This process of deviation began with Banu Umaiyyah and continues today under the Saudi regime. The nation-States established in the Muslim world by the colonial powers and their 'Muslim' agents are also designed to make our political deviation permanent.

Some 15 years ago we in the Muslim Institute set out to discover those in the *Ummah*, both *ulama* and ordinary Muslims, who would be prepared to participate in the task of research to determine the area within Islam where those suffering from internal error and deviation would be prepared to converge. Our instinct told us that the one single *Ummah*[2] could only be superficially and temporarily divided. Another instinctive hypothesis that guided us was that the error and subsequent divisions in the *Ummah* were primarily political and, therefore, temporary. This meant that the process of correction and convergence would have to be led either by the rewriting of Muslim political thought or by the 'big bang' effect of a major political event. We were naïve enough to postulate that we could rewrite Muslim political thought and to hope that, some day, our formulations might generate a major political event.[3]

History, as we now know, had other ideas. Islam, despite error and deviations within it, is such a powerful system of beliefs and ideas that it was bound to produce its own answer to the ills of the *Ummah*. We should have known all along that Islam, if it was the Whole Truth from Allah, would also include within it the capacity to generate corrective processes at crucial moments in history. Before the coming of the last Prophet, upon whom be peace, this was done by successive prophets who appeared at intervals. Now the role of correction and convergence is performed by non-prophetic agents, such as individuals, movements and revolutions. Once motivated and activated by the historical situation, the corrective agents must have the power to move the entire body of Muslims, the *Ummah*, towards convergence at a central point within Islam. In recent times a number of individuals, and the movements they inspired, have tried unsuccessfully to emerge in the role of the central corrective agents, but failed. Among these were Hasan al-Banna (founder of Al-Ikhwan al-Muslimoon) and Mawlana Abul Ala Mawdoodi (founder of the Jama'at-e Islami). It would seem that the role of the central corrective agent can only be performed by the Islamic State. Those who failed, failed precisely because they could not establish the Islamic State. The act of establishing the Islamic State would appear to be necessary for a successful transition to the role of the central corrective agent to end error and deviation within the *Ummah*.

Support for this view is found in the *Sirah* of Prophet Muhammad, upon whom be peace. As an individual in Makkah the role of the Prophet was limited to bringing a handful of individuals to Islam. Yet even while in Makkah the Prophet sought and found State protection for his small band of followers. This is the significance of the migration of many early Muslims from Makkah to Abyssinia. Once, after the *hijra* to Medina, Islam had undergone transition to Statehood, the spread of Islam to the peninsula was rapid and total. Islam is incomplete without the Islamic State; there is no room for dispute on this point. It has far-reaching implications for the *da'wah* work undertaken by well-meaning Muslims, as well as for the *da'wah* work into which the energies of Muslims are being diverted today by those committed to the *status quo*. The Saudi regime in particular spends vast amounts of money on *da'wah* in order to absorb the energies of many Muslims throughout the world and to divert them into dead-end activity. But the chief instrument of *da'wah* is the Islamic State; *da'wah* without the Islamic State is like an invitation without an address.

The political nature of Islam and the Prophethood of Muhammad, upon whom be peace, was clearly understood by the Quraish of Makkah from the beginning. When the Quraish approached him with a 'deal' they also offered him kingship. The delegation of the Quraish was led by Utbah bin Rabiah. The incident is documented in all books of *Sirah*. The goal of Muhammad's Prophethood was not his personal power or kingship, but the transformation of the area into an Islamic State. Many years later Makkah fell to Islam as the result of a military expedition mounted by the Prophet from the Islamic State that had been consolidated around Medina. It is the Islamic State that bears the main responsibility for *da'wah*.

The point that is obscured in modern, apologetic literature of Islam, and neatly side-stepped by the orientalists, is that Islam is not only a message, Islam is also a method. The message of Islam carried by the methods of pacifist Christian missionaries is unlikely to yield the desired results. Such an approach may help to turn Islam into a ritualised religion, but it cannot achieve the goals of Islam. The complete message of Islam includes the method of Islam. This is why there is so much emphasis in Islam on the *Sunnah* and the *Sirah* of the Prophet Muhammad, upon whom be peace. And this is why the procedures and the historical processes required to establish the Islamic State are inseparable parts of Islam. Islam, therefore, is incomplete without the Islamic State.

The 'Islamic parties' that emerged during the colonial period often did not grasp this essential point. They understood and presented Islam within the framework of European-style social democracy. For them the Islamic State was only a slightly updated and 'Islamised' version of the post-colonial nation-State. It only required them to win an election and 'come to power'. These 'Islamic' political parties did not realise that there was a colonial legacy to be undone and dismantled. In their simplistic thinking the 'Islamic State' of their conception would be built on the secular and nationalist foundations of the colonial independent State. It is undoubtedly true is that some of these political parties had perhaps unwittingly borrowed many of their ideas from sources outside Islam.[4]

The 'act' of establishing the Islamic State itself comes at the end of a prolonged process of corrective action amongst those 'lost' within Islam. In the Sunni tradition, one must admit, this corrective process has still hardly begun. Political thought in the Sunni tradition is still lost in the diversions caused by the 'Islamic parties', Arab nationalism, the Khilafat movement in India, and the easy availability of political patronage for most of the last 1400 years.

In the Shi'i tradition, on the other hand, the first significant step in the right direction was taken early in their history, as rejection of compromise with existing political systems. Its roots go back to the rejection of Yazid's authority by Imam Husain and his subsequent *shahadah* at Karbala. The next major corrective step came many centuries later, after Iran had been converted to the Shi'i school of thought in the early part of the sixteenth century. It appeared as a debate among the Shi'i *ulama* on what seemed to be a technical matter. This debate, in the second half of the eighteenth century, was between two groups of *ulama* known as *usuli* and *akhbari*. The *akhbari* (or communicators) held the view that, during the *ghaiba* (occultation) of the Twelfth Imam, it is not permissible for religious scholars to engage in the use of reason to enact a certain judgement, to apply the principles of the law to a specific problem or situation. All that could be done was merely to have recourse to *hadith* (hence the name *akhbari*), and by sifting *hadith* reach a conclusion about any particular issue. This school tended towards a total abolition of the discipline of jurisprudence. The *usuli ulama*, on the other hand, held that, during the absence of the Twelfth Imam, it was permissible to engage in independent reasoning. One qualified to do so was the *mujtahid*: he who uses his reason guided by principles of the *shari'ah* to make decisions acting upon which the general body of Muslims could solve their problems. All Muslims who are not *mujtahids* must follow the guidance of one who is. This is known as *taqlid*. The senior *mujtahids*, who came to be followed by large numbers of Shi'i Muslims, were called *maraje'* (singular *marja'* or *marja'-i taqlid*). The argument was won by *usuli ulama* and the *akhbari* position was abandoned. Hamid Algar points out that 'the Revolution in Iran, at least the particular shape that it has taken, the form of leadership that it has enjoyed and continues to enjoy, would also be unthinkable without the triumph of the *usuli* position... in the eighteenth century.'[5]

The emergence of the *usuli ulama* can be described as the development of a self-correcting mechanism within the Shi'i tradition. How important this was for the world of Islam as a whole is only just beginning to become apparent. In the first phase of this self-correcting process, two things have happened: first the doors of *ijtihad* were thrown open; and second, there emerged *ulama*, the *maraje'-i-taqlid*, who often exercised greater influence, even power, than many rulers. For all practical purposes the *maraje'* came to represent an 'Islamic State' within the larger territorial State. The traditional Shi'i position, that all political power in the absence of the Twelfth Imam was illegitimate and should not be sought, was deep-rooted and the *maraje'* functioned within the umbrella of the Qajar dynasty that had replaced the Safavis in 1795. Throughout this period, from 1795 to the Islamic Revolution in 1979, the primary concern of the *ulama* of Iran was to limit the inevitable illegitimacy of the existing government. It was in this framework that Mirza Hasan Shirazi gave his famous *fatwa* (1892) on the consumption of tobacco in Iran being *haram* if its production and marketing were undertaken by a British monopoly. The *ulama*'s participation in the Constitutional Revolution in Iran (1905-1909) was also made possible by the wider concerns of the *usuli* school.

The otherwise powerful *usuli* establishment suffered from two weaknesses. The first was the senior *ulama*'s self-imposed abstinence from seeking ultimate political authority; and the second was the multiplicity of the *maraje'*. At any one time a number of Grand Ayatullahs claimed large followings, and often competed among themselves for followers (*muqallidin*). The two handicaps are closely linked. So long as the *ulama* did not contemplate the exercise of supreme political power there was no need for a single leader, and so long as there was no single leader, a kind of *marja'* of the *maraje'*, the exercise of ultimate political authority could not be contemplated. These self-inflicted disabilities appeared so entrenched in Shi'i theology that the ruling classes, the dynasties (the Pehlavi since 1926) and their British and American backers, did not feel threatened from Qum. But the *usuli* revolution had also opened the doors of *ijtihad*. It was only a matter of time before the process of *ijtihad*, begun by *usuli ulama*, led to the ultimate step, in terms of Shi'i theology, of setting up the Islamic State in the absence of the Twelfth Imam. This is what we have come to call the Islamic Revolution in Iran.

The Sunni *ulama*, equally 'lost' within Islam, have still not begun the long and painful task of clearing away the debris of their failures, recovering from their self-inflicted disabilities, and breaking the habit of supine obedience to patronising rulers. At the moment the worldwide network of 'court *ulama*' who serve the Saudi regime (and other secular governments) are the most error-ridden and deviant body of people lost within Islam. If the Sunni *ulama* would only lift the veil of their prejudice, they should see that Imam Khomeini has brought the Shi'i caravan back to the point where we all started in the first place. In a *fatwa* issued on January 6, 1988, Imam Khomeini said that Islamic government represents 'absolute sovereign power as delegated by Allah *subhanahu wa ta'ala* to the Prophet, upon whom be peace'. This, said Imam Khomeini, 'is the most important of Divine precepts (*ahkam*) and takes precedence over all the other secondary Divine precepts'. Imam Khomeini added: 'If the powers of Islamic government are to be confined within the framework of secondary Divine precepts, then the form of Divine rule and absolute sovereignty as delegated to the Prophet, upon whom be peace, would be a senseless and hollow phenomenon. ' If this was so, he added, the legislative and administrative powers of Islamic government would be severely restricted. Imam Khomeini went on to give several examples of legislative, administrative, military and economic policies that would be impossible to implement if the Islamic government was bound by secondary Divine precepts. These included the acquisition of private property for major public works, such as new roads, compulsory military service, foreign trade, prohibition of hoarding, customs and excise, taxation and fair pricing of goods and services. Imam Khomeini then argued that 'Islamic government which is part of the absolute sovereign power of Allah, Prophet, upon whom be peace, is one of the primary precepts of Islam and takes precedence over all the secondary precepts'. The concept that the political power exercised by the Prophet must be inherited in full by rulers who follow him has always been clear in Sunni thought. This is exactly how the *rashidoon khulafah* understood the source of their authority. The Islamic State is only an extension of the authority of the leader, who is a *khalifah* (*na'ib* or vicegerent) of the Prophet. This *fatwa* from Imam Khomeini[6] has completed the long process of corrective action within the Shi'i school that had been at the very heart of the *akhbari/ usuli* controversy. It should be noted that some residual influence of the *akhbari* position still persists not only in Iran but to a much greater degree among the Shi'i *ulama* of Iraq, India, Pakistan and Bahrain and among their followers. The leading edge of Shi'i political thought, that of Imam Khomeini and his close associates, has emerged only since the death of Ayatullah Burujirdi in March 1962. It was only then that Ayatullah Khomeini began to give lectures on political issues critical of the Shah and exploring the possibility of government by *mujtahid*s. He was repeatedly arrested during 1963 and exiled to Turkey the following year. In 1965 he moved to Najaf, the great centre of Shi'i learning in Iraq. It was during a course of lectures on Islamic government delivered there in 1970 that he developed the concept of *vilayat-i faqih*. With his *fatwa* of January 6, 1988, it is probably no exaggeration to say that Imam Khomeini corrected the political deviation of the entire *Ummah* that began with the advent of the Umaiyyad rule. In terms of the legitimacy of the leadership of the Islamic State, Imam Khomeini restored the situation as it existed during the rule of Ali Ibn Abi Talib, the fourth of the *rashidoon khulafah*. This means that, for all practical purposes, in terms of State and politics in Islam, the *Ummah* has been returned to a point very close to the time of the Prophet Muhammad, upon whom be peace.

During this very short period, from 1962 to 1990, history has moved at an extraordinary pace. Students of history are familiar with the leapfrogging relationship that exists between political ideas and political events. At times ideas run far ahead of events, and at other times events shape ideas. For example, the great *usuli* school that challenged and eventually defeated the *akhbari* orthodoxy in Shi'i thought can be traced back to Allama Hilli (Jamaluddin Abu Mansur Hasan ibn Yusuf) in the fourteenth century. From the time of his death in 1325 to the triumph of the *usuli* ideas in Iran in the eighteenth century the pace of change was slow. In the nineteenth century in Iran the *usuli ulama*, especially the *maraje'*, began to influence political events.[7] From 1978-79 until now virtually all political thought, Shi'i and Sunni, has been shaped by the events in Iran. The ideas and followers of Imam Khomeini are pushing the frontiers of *usuli* thought towards a total convergence of all political thought in Islam. It is possible that Imam Khomeini, like Allama Hilli before him, was himself not aware of all the wider implications of his ideas and *ijtihad*. It is almost certainly the case that the interpretation of the Imam's *fatwa* on January 6, 1988, will be long debated by Shi'i and Sunni *ulama*, both inside and outside Iran.

However, at present and for the limited purpose of the argument developed in this paper, the realisation that politically one part of the *Ummah* at least has achieved a position that puts it within two or three decades of the Prophet is an exhilarating experience. We are liberated from the responsibility for at least some parts of our history. We can shed the guilt that haunts us for belonging to a tradition of continuous error and deviation. We can stop having to defend or justify what goes by the name of 'Islamic history' and dynastic *malukiyyah*. We can also 'black box'[8] a great deal of the divisive theology written and promoted during this period. This would allow a new kind of *usuli* revolution to spread to all schools of thought in Islam and to open up the doors of *ijtihad* in all traditions of thought. We can once again begin to feel historically close to the Prophet, upon whom be peace. This newly achieved proximity, though largely a matter of perception, establishes new spiritual and intellectual links with the *Sirah* and the *Sunnah* of Muhammad, upon whom be peace.

Once we place ourselves within this time-frame close to the Prophet, virtually all subsequent sources of error and deviation in the *Ummah* disappear. The disabilities imposed by our long fruitless commitment to essentially indefensible positions also fade away. Or at least the option of liberating ourselves from such historical handicaps is now available. Imam Khomeini had to endure resistance from conservative Shi'i *ulama* on his original *ijtihad* of the *vali-i faqih's* rulership in the absence of the Twelfth Imam. His decree that the *vali-i faqih* is the *khalifah* (*na'ib*) of the Prophet and that the Islamic State, too, enjoys the same powers as conferred upon the Prophet by Allah *subhanahu wa ta'ala* wipes the slate clean for all Muslims, especially the *ulama*. Once this position is taken up, it does not matter whether one is Sunni or Shi'i. All positions within Islam are valid and true, but none more so than the position that takes us closest to the Prophet's time, especially a position that enables us to establish a Leadership (and a State) that derives its authority as the *khalifah* (vicegerent) of the Prophet, upon whom be peace. Such is the capacity to generate self-corrective processes that exists within Islam.

But the process that leads to corrective action needs better understanding. Error and deviation within Islam soon begin to accumulate unacceptable results. It was this accumulation of unacceptable results that must have sparked off the *akhbari/usuli* controversy among the Shi'i *ulama* more than two centuries ago. The triumph of the *usuli* position clearly corrected most errors of earlier *ijtihad*, but not all. However, the opening of the doors to further and more fundamental *ijtihad* led to the emergence of *maraje'* who filled the vacuum of leadership caused by the occultation of the Twelfth Imam. Once the role of leadership had been taken up by a small number of *maraje'*, they were set on a course that would eventually produce a single leader. But a single leader in Islam is only possible within the framework of the political power of Islam established in the Islamic State. If the corrective process begun by the *usuli ulama* was to continue, then the eventual emergence of a single *marja'* as the *marja'* of the *maraje'*, was inevitable. And this could happen only within the framework of what we now call the Islamic Revolution in Iran, or the act of establishing the Islamic State. The process of *ijtihad* that preceded the Islamic Revolution, and the emergence of an Islamic State led by a *vali-i faqih*, produced, within ten years, a *fatwa* from Imam Khomeini to the effect that he, as *vali-i faqih*, and the Islamic State exercise authority as *khalifah* or *na'ib* of the Prophet Muhammad, upon whom be peace.

The Imam's latest *fatwa* could only come after the new Islamic State had experienced the difficulty, indeed the impossibility, of performing its proper executive, legislative and judicial functions without the ultimate source of authority and power in Islam as *khalifah* of the Prophet. The absence of such authority from the *vali-i faqih* and the Islamic State was clearly an error, and the results of such error soon accumulated and were found to be unacceptable. In a sense the authority as *khalifah* already existed but had not been claimed or clearly understood. The Imam then made the authority explicit and unambiguous. Imam Khomeini did not, for reasons that can be guessed, put in so many words, but the fact is that he became then *khilafatur-Rasool*, or vicegerent of the Prophet, upon whom be peace. We can now safely assume that the demise of what Dr Ali Shari'ati called Safavid Shi'ism is now all but complete, though some irritant traces of it in Shi'i rituals and culture will persist for some time. We have also seen that the act of establishing the Islamic State is the most powerful corrective agent in Islam. This is because, in the political process, even small errors soon lead to large and visible results that are clearly unacceptable. What this means is that error in matter of theology affects rituals and *ibadah* and can persist for a long time, or even for ever, without causing harm to Islam or the *Ummah*. Perhaps it is also true that within Islam a wide range of variations is possible in peripheral areas of *fiqh*. These variations do not amount to error or deviation. In actual error are those who allow such peripheral areas of *fiqh* to cause heated debate and controversy among Muslims. In itself this diversity in Islamic practices does not usually lead to cumulative results that reach unacceptable levels. But this may happen in conditions where error and deviation on larger issues of leadership, State and politics in Islam reach dangerous levels, leading in turn to the disintegration of the *Ummah*. In conditions of extreme disintegration, such as those prevailing in parts of the *Ummah* today, these peripheral issues may also cause bloodshed. This is why the existence of any kind of Muslim ruler, including *malukiyyah* for the greater part of our history, did not allow peripheral issues to cause bloodshed on a large scale. In India, for instance, open and bloody conflict between Shi'i and Sunni Muslims was unknown during the Mogal rule. In recent years the disintegration of the polity in Pakistan has reached a similar stage, causing bloody conflicts among Muslims. It is widely suspected that the post-colonial secular rulers in Muslim nation-States deliberately create such conflicts to divert attention from the convergence of Islamic thought in matters of leadership, State and politics. This also explains the relentless propaganda against the Shi'i school of thought that has been unleashed by the West generally and by the secular Muslim rulers in particular. They know that their only chance of survival lies in their ability to obstruct and abort Islam's processes of corrective action, preventing them from reaching the Sunni areas of the *Ummah*.

The fact is that the process of correction of error and deviation within the Shi'i tradition is now almost complete, at least so far as Iran is concerned. Some parts of Shi'i opinion outside Iran are suspicious of the changes that Imam Khomeini's *ijtihad* has achieved. It is also known that within Iran there are *ulama* who have deep reservations. However, these are unlikely to halt the powerful forces of internally-generated corrective action. We must now outline in brief the degree of error and deviation within Islam that is found in the Sunni tradition. The Sunni political experience is, of course, very different. For the Sunni Muslims there was no vacuum of leadership, only a gradual decline in its quality. The Sunni school recognises the pre-eminence of the first four *rashidoon khulafah*. The qualitative change that occurred when Mu'awia ibn Abi Sufyan became, in his own words, the first *malik* (king) of the Muslims, is also known and recognised. There is no difference between the Shi'i and Sunni understanding of the events and issues that led to Imam Husain's *shahadah* (martyrdom) at Karbala. The root of political error and subsequent deviation in the Sunni school lies in the easy acceptance and almost automatic *bay'ah* that was given to rulers of known political deficiency and moral corruption. This happened because opposition to the established ruler came to be regarded a greater *fitna* than the ruler's known deviation from the classical standards of private and moral excellence laid down in Islam. This gave many Sunni activists easy access to the courts of the rulers and to political patronage. Under these circumstances, and so long as Muslim rulers wielded considerable power and presided over vast empires, there was little pressure to re-examine established positions. The vastness of the Islamic empire and civilisation, the emergence of large cities and seats of learning, and the political dominance of the world of Islam over all else, lulled Sunni Muslims into a false sense of security and self-righteousness. The initial error and deviation from Islam that *malukiyyah* represented was hidden by the rapid expansion and success of the political power of the Muslim States. The initial thrust that was given to the political history of the Muslims by the Prophet, upon whom be peace, and the *rashidoon khulafah* was used by subsequent rulers to hide their own error and deviation. It was inevitable, therefore, that eventually the error and deviation heralded by *malukiyyah* would multiply and lead Muslim society inexorably towards moral decay and political and military decline. This decline was not obvious so long as Muslim armies kept the enemies of Islam at bay or recovered any ground that was lost, such as the recapture of Jerusalem from the Christians by Salah al-Din Ayyubi.

The full extent of the cumulative damage that had been caused to Dar al-Islam during hundreds of years of progressive decline and decay under *malukiyyah* became obvious when the European powers began to emerge in their imperialist role. In a hundred years or so before the defeat of the Uthmaniyyah State in the 1914-18 war, virtually the whole of the world of Islam had passed into European hands. After 1919 the European powers consolidated their hold on the Arab heartland of Islam by dividing it up into client States. Mustafa Kemal completed the demolition of the last political remnant of *Dar al-Islam* by formally abolishing the *khilafah* in 1924. The cumulative effect of initial error and deviation had reached its logical conclusion and Islam had lost all semblance of political and military presence in the affairs of mankind. No result could be more unacceptable. But the habit of supine obedience that the Sunni *ulama* had cultivated during several centuries was not to be abandoned at once. Even the realisation that a catastrophe had overtaken them has been slow to emerge. Apart from the popular emotions stirred by the Khilafat Movement in India during 1919-22, there was little reaction among the Sunni *ulama*. Their immediate response appears to have been in line with their traditional role. They busied themselves with trying to seek political patronage from the new political order - from the new Saudi 'kingdom' in the tradition of *malukiyyah*, and from the new nation-States, and even from the colonial States. These rulers were only too anxious to provide these *ulama* with a sense of security and political patronage in return for political subservience. The two men who made valiant but futile attempts to revive the political fortunes of Islam were Hasan al-Banna and Abul Ala Mawdoodi. Notably, neither was a traditional *alim*.

They and their parties, Al-Ikhwan al-Muslimoon and the Jama'at-e Islami, also ended up on the side of the *status quo*, enjoying extensive and lucrative patronage from Saudi Arabia. Even the 'Islamic State' of their conception differed little from the welfare-oriented, liberal and democratic States of Europe. With little or no support from the Sunni *ulama*, such attempts did not amount to much. We have to admit that the kind of corrective action that began with the success of the *usuli* school among the Shi'i *ulama* has yet to begin in the Sunni tradition. It can be argued that the nature and degree of error and deviation in the Shi'i school was different from those in the Sunni school. There is weight in this argument. But there are three common features that should be noted without attempting to find their sources in theological formulations. These are:

1. The *akhbari* ulama during the Safavid dynasty in Iran (1502-1747) were as open to political manipulation by the rulers as Sunni *ulama* at any time in history, including the modern period.

2. The error and deviance in the Shi'i school had left Shi'i *ulama* politically as ineffective as the Sunni *ulama* of today.

3. The Shi'i *ulama*, before the *usuli* revolution, had closed the doors on *ijtihad* as firmly as the Sunni *ulama* have done up to the present time.

The revolution in Iran would not be possible without the prior clearing up, through *ijtihad*, of a number of issues peculiar to Shi'i theology. It is beyond the scope of this paper to list the issues awaiting *ijtihad* by Sunni *ulama*. Nor is it possible to speculate about what it would take for an intellectual movement to emerge in the Sunni school comparable in scope and extent to the *usuli* movement in the Shi'i school. Many in the Sunni school would argue that their deviation was only an error of judgement that led to compromise with *malukiyyah*. Be that as it may, the fact is that the effect of that compromise on Sunni political thought and behaviour has been devastating. The result is that most Sunni *ulama* today suffer from all the failures of understanding of political issues that were common among *akhbari* Shi'i *ulama* before the *usuli* revolution.

The modern *malukiyyah*, represented by the Saudi 'royal family', and all the other secular, nationalist regimes that rule over colonial-style nation-States in Sunni areas, would dearly like the Sunni *ulama* to wait for an *usuli* revolution of their own. This would give the rulers a comfortable breathing-space of at least two hundred years; long enough, in their view, for the secular culture and civilisation of their choice to take root and to destroy the influence of Islam on succeeding generations. The Sunni *ulama* must avoid this trap at all costs. There are several good reasons for not waiting for an *usuli* revolution in the Sunni school. There is no reason to believe that every part of the *Ummah* has to undergo a similar experience before error and deviation can be corrected. The Shi'i *ulama* of two hundred years ago did not have the advantage of having seen and experienced an Islamic Revolution in another part of the *Ummah*. They had to generate corrective action from within the Shi'i school; hence the *usuli* commitment to *ijtihad*. In addition, two hundred years ago, while the Shi'i *ulama* had experienced the total absence of political power, the Sunni *ulama* had not yet experienced the total collapse of what they regarded as the Islamic State. Today the Sunni school has not only experienced the total absence of the centralized power of Islam, it has also experienced prolonged political subservience of all parts of the *Ummah* to *kufr*. The business of terminating the dominance of *kufr* over Islam and the *Ummah* is too urgent to require an intellectual revolution to precede it. Finally, perhaps one *usuli* revolution in any one part of the *Ummah* is enough for all parts of the *Ummah*. This is because the corrective process within Islam, once started, must lead those engaged in it to common ground in Islam acceptable to all Muslims. It would not be a corrective process in Islam if it were to stop at the boundaries of a particular school of thought.

In the case of Iran we have seen that, for a long time, *ijtihad* by *usuli ulama* only affected issues most commonly identified with the Shi'i school. Later the same process became Islamic rather than Shi'i. When the Islamic movement in Iran mounted its assault to bring down *malukiyyah*, the final act of establishing the Islamic State had begun. The final stages of transition from the Islamic movement to the Islamic State have been called the Islamic Revolution. The demands of the Islamic movement and the Islamic State are such that these stages cannot be negotiated successfully by those adhering to a single school of thought. The act of establishing the Islamic State is such a liberating experience that all other boundaries within Islam become irrelevant and insignificant. At first this realisation comes only to the senior leadership, while the rank and file celebrate the victory of their own school of thought. The Islamic State, therefore, cannot be a 'Shi'i' or a 'Sunni' State. Either it is an Islamic State or it is not. To be an Islamic State it must be acceptable as such to all Muslims; and, to be acceptable to all Muslims, the leader of the State must rule as the *khalifah* or *na'ib* of the Prophet, upon whom be peace. That was the point of the *fatwa* of Imam Khomeini on January 6, 1988.

With this *fatwa*, Imam Khomeini has sent a clear message to the *Ummah* at large that, whatever the Shi'i origins of the long process leading to the Islamic Revolution, the State that has been established in Iran is 'Islamic' within the meaning of the term as it is understood by Muslims of all schools of thought in Islam. This *fatwa* of the Imam represents another Revolution within the Shi'i school. Imam Khomeini's *fatwa* also confirmed the view of the Islamic Revolution that we in the Muslim Institute have held from the beginning. It was our view in 1980 that the first Islamic State, established after such a long gap in history, would be a 'primitive model' of the ideal.[9] And so it has proved. The corrective process within Islam has continued during the early years of the new Islamic State. In the next phase one would expect the Islamic State of Iran to begin to take a broader view of the historical situation from the point of view of the *Ummah* and the global Islamic movement. In the first decade after the Revolution, the bureaucracy of the Islamic State has remained largely 'Irani' and 'national' in outlook, and the *ulama* have concentrated their attention on cultivating the traditional Shi'i connections outside Iran. But the senior leadership, especially Imam Khomeini and Ayatullah Montazeri, have spoken of the *Ummah*, the global Islamic movement and the need for world Islamic Revolution in ringing terms. This was a constant theme of Imam Khomeini's speeches and messages. His message, on the occasion of *Hajj*, 1407, deals with this subject in great detail and runs to more than 20,000 words. The English text was published in *Kayhan International*, August 1, 1987. In the decade that lies ahead, State policy should increasingly begin to reflect the vision of the senior leadership.

History has now reached a point where it is possible to draw a simple diagram to represent it:

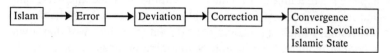

For slightly greater detail, the same diagram may be drawn to show the separate progressions of the Shi'i and Sunni schools:

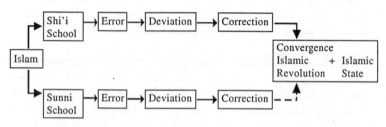

It would be futile, indeed quite wrong, to attempt to identify actual points of error or degrees of deviation in the two great schools of thought in Islam. What is obvious, however, is that in the Shi'i school the corrective process began with the *usuli* revolution and the result is not only the convergence of thought but also the emergence of the Islamic State. In the Sunni school there have been numerous attempts at correction. The most recent of these were by the two best-known 'Islamic parties', Al-Ikhwan al-Muslimoon and the Jama'at-e Islami. Neither represented the kind of *usuli* rethinking of fundamental issues achieved by the Shi'i *ulama*. The Ikhwan and the Jama'at were purely political responses; they failed to break out of the stranglehold of modern political thought. The Shi'i *ulama*, leading the Muslim *Ummah* in Iran, have also established a living, dynamic, versatile, powerful and *muttaqi* Islamic State through an Islamic Revolution. The area of convergence, defined and developed into an Islamic State, is now acting like a magnet on the political thought and action of all Muslims. It is now impossible for anyone to think of politics and political issues in Islam without reference to the Islamic State of Iran. On the political compass of Islam the needle now points firmly towards Iran. Every Muslim has to read his position with respect to the Islamic Revolution. No part of the *Ummah* is outside the influence of the Islamic Revolution and the new Islamic State.

The situation affects Iran as well as the entire *Ummah*. Neither Iran nor the *Ummah* can escape from this relationship. Its implications are profound and should be discussed at length. But first we must return to Bahira, the Christian monk of Busra, and Waraqa, the Makkan Christian. Because of their knowledge of the Christian scripture, and their observation of the historical situation, they were expecting a new prophet. Clearly a long-term commitment to history and historical trends is a major source of knowledge. The totality of knowledge available to mankind at any one point in time is a historical phenomenon. For instance, it would not be possible to write about error, deviation, correction and convergence without the advantage of history we now enjoy. Similarly, it was not possible for Imam Khomeini to give the *fatwa* of January 6, 1988, without the accumulation of unacceptable results through nine years of experience of Islamic government. It is only now possible for us to postulate that the experience of convergence, described above, has made it possible for the *Ummah* to place itself within two or three decades of the era of the Prophet, upon whom be peace. The *akhbari* school in the Shi'i tradition did not realise that they were 'wrong' until the accumulation of unacceptable results gave rise to the *usuli ulama*. Once the *usuli ulama* had taken over the leadership of the Shi'i school of thought, it was also inevitable that they would eventually claim the Prophet's *khilafah* and the right to set up an Islamic State in the absence of the Twelfth Imam. It is now obvious that the 'correct' or 'right' position in Islam should always take the *Ummah* close to the Prophet and the *rashidoon khulafah*. In history time is not static; nor is human experience. A combination of the two, the passage of time and human experience over time, enriches our knowledge and understanding of Islam and of history, past and future.

Once a cycle of error, deviation, correction and convergence has been completed in any one part of the *Ummah*, or in any one school of thought in Islam, the knowledge thus generated should be acceptable to all schools of thought in Islam and to the entire *Ummah*. The validity of the newly expanded base of our knowledge will remain uncertain and problematic unless it is demonstrated that the historical sequence from which it is derived is repeatable. Historical sequences are repeatable over long periods of time. Thus, if the Islamic Revolution in Iran has not been followed by another revolution within a decade or two in any other part of the *Ummah*, it may not necessarily mean that the first Islamic Revolution's validity is in doubt. However, if another fifty or a hundred years pass without evidence of repeatability, then the validity of the historical sequence achieved in Iran would begin to lose its wider relevance. Similarly, if the accretion of new knowledge from the process of correction and convergence remains confined to the Shi'i school and does not become relevant to all schools of thought in Islam, then the process may also lose its wider relevance. The failure to repeat itself outside Iran, or failure to attract wider acceptance in the other schools of thought in Islam, may also suggest that the process of correction and convergence is in some respects incomplete. Should this be the case, new evidence of unacceptable results will accumulate. However, if predictable and desirable results begin to emerge in other parts of the *Ummah*, then the validity of the process of correction and convergence will have been established.

It is clear that, just as error and deviation accumulate unacceptable results, so the successful completion of a process of correction and convergence must be identifiable with reference to the original historical experience of Islam. For instance, in the original historical experience of Islam the Quraish of Makkah repeatedly invaded the fledgling Islamic State in Medina. It can even be argued that the Quraish invaded Medina to prevent it from becoming established as an Islamic State, and that this high level of persistent conflict with a hostile environment helped greatly in the consolidation of the political and military power of Islam in Medina, and subsequently all over the Arab Peninsula. This would indicate that a high level of persistent conflict with its external enemies for a long time is an indispensable part of the experience of the Islamic State. Should the traditional enemies of Islam fail to react as the Quraish of Makkah did, it can safely be assumed that no Islamic State is in fact being set up. This would fit in with our view of the Muslim nation-States that not only were they not invaded by *kufr*, but were actively helped to become established. This failure of the 'independent' post-colonial States to provoke the enemies of Islam into belligerence is clearly because these Muslim nation-States were in fact created to serve the global purposes of *kufr*. All subsequent events were equally predictable. The Arab States' open complicity with the United States and the Soviet

Union in the invasion of Iran falls into this category of predictable and desirable events that must follow the establishment of an Islamic State. We can also predict that the vast military superiority of *kufr* and its allies, the *munafiqoon*, will eventually be defeated, just as the Quraish were defeated in the original historical experience of Islam. If Iran had not been invaded and subjected to a concerted attempt to destabilise it by the superpowers of *kufr* and their allies, then we would have to doubt whether the Revolution and the State there were in fact 'Islamic'.

Thus history provides us with a set of rules by which to judge the true nature of historical events. It is clear that States set up by colonial powers, or otherwise protected and 'guaranteed' by the superpowers of *kufr*, cannot be 'Islamic' as well. This also applies to States whose rulers are attempting to duplicate, imitate or simulate the European nationalist, democratic, capitalist or communist models of 'progress' and 'development'. Most of these States also receive economic and military 'aid' from *kafir* patrons. All these States, which at present means all States in the Muslim areas of the world except Iran, are not only un-Islamic but also in fact actively opposed to Islam. What this tells us is that the political map of the *Ummah* today represents extremes of error and grossly compounded deviation from the political norms of Islam. In other words, the political map of the *Ummah* today represents the grand total of unacceptable results accumulated over many hundreds of years of political error and deviation. Perhaps we should not hesitate to admit further that this grand total of unacceptable results of history represents the Sunni school's initial error and its grossly compounded deviation over nearly 1400 years. The Sunni school's compromise with *malukiyyah* and political corruption represents the greatest single instance of error and deviation within Islam. Some Sunni Muslims would argue that the Shi'i error in effectively suspending major precepts of Islam concerning State, politics and leadership in the absence (*ghaiba*) of the Twelfth Imam was a greater error. Perhaps, but the impact of the Shi'i error on the *Ummah* was limited and has proved relatively easy to correct; the Sunni school's compromise with *malukiyyah*, and more recently with western political thought, has played havoc with the political fortunes of the entire *Ummah*. This error and its compounded deviation have led the *Ummah* to worldwide political and military defeat. It is the failure of the Sunnis to respond to history's devastating verdict on their political record that has made the entire *Ummah* subservient to *kufr*. Almost none of this blame can be put at the door of Shi'i error and deviation. Yet, despite this overwhelming evidence of unacceptable results in all parts of the *Ummah*, large numbers of Sunni *ulama* remain attached to the Saudi *malukiyyah* even today. Other Sunni groups, especially those who tried to form political parties, remain close to nationalist and secular democratic 'ideals' of the colonial period.

Be that as it may, it is not desirable to compare the relative qualities of error and deviation and their impact. All that is important is what we have already noted: that the 'correct' or 'right' position in Islam will always be close to the Prophet, upon whom be peace, and close to the *rashidoon khulafah*. The completed cycle of error, deviation, correction and convergence has already brought the Shi'i school to the 'correct' or 'right' position in Islam. However, for the validity of their achievement the Shi'i school must now persuade the Sunni school to accept their results as desirable and repeatable. For this to happen, a group of *ulama*, drawn from both the principal schools of thought in Islam, must come together. In the Shi'i school this means that some of the *ulama* closest to the Islamic State of Iran, especially those who were closest to Imam Khomeini, must come forward to explain their new position to the Sunni *ulama*. From the Sunni school we need those *ulama* who have little or no contact with the current deviant and corrupt systems. The first step must be the coming together of a group of Sunni *ulama* who understand the need to learn from the Shi'i experience of correction and convergence. These Sunni *ulama* must be those who accept that the Shi'i position after the Islamic Revolution in Iran is now substantially no different from what the classical Sunni position was before their own error and deviation into *malukiyyah*. Such Sunni *ulama* will help to transfer the new knowledge and experience developed in the Shi'i school to all parts of the *Ummah*. The great advantage the Shi'i school now enjoys is not theological. Indeed, the argument presented here is entirely non-theological. Its root and source is history, the movement and direction of history, the impact of history, the Muslims' response to history, and above all the expectation of future historical events. This is why we began with Bahira and Waraqa.

History is a crucible. It is relentless and impartial in dealing with error and deviation. History is intolerant of all degrees of perversion of the truth, however well-meaning and sincere the human motive behind it. All kinds of religious traditions have fallen into the trap of exaggerated self-righteousness and absurd claims of having discovered the whole truth to the exclusion of all others. A failure to check actual results against the promised and desired goals leads to the degeneration of behaviour and the erosion of morality. This in turn leads to a garrison mentality, with fragmentary groups claiming that the whole truth lies on their side of the barricade. History is contemptuous of those who indulge in this type of puerility. With time, history develops a profile of deviation and half-truths and contrasts it with the whole truth. History converts mental, spiritual, moral, political and theological half-truths into hard facts. These historical facts in time lead to the accumulation of results that are not only unacceptable, but also ugly and deeply humiliating.

The crucible of history has reduced every part of the *Ummah* to our present condition of dismemberment and subservience to *kufr*. The ugly and humiliating facts that stare us in the face are the nation-States created by western colonial powers in Muslim areas of the world. Even more ugly and humiliating is the political, economic and cultural domination that the western civilisation has acquired over the lands and peoples of Islam. The ugliest of all spectacles is the corruption of the present rulers and ruling classes in the world of Islam. Perhaps the deepest cut of all is the inability of Sunni *ulama* to challenge the *status quo*. The correction and convergence that the Shi'i *ulama* of Iran have achieved is still a partial and incomplete historical movement. History will respond and deliver the goods only if the sequence of correction and convergence is repeated in all parts of the *Ummah*.

NOTES:

1. Except by such minor groups as the Bahais of Iran and the Ahmadiyyahs of India and Pakistan, regarded by all Muslims as *kuffar*.

2. Al-Qur'an, 21:92.

3. See the *Draft Prospectus* of the Muslim Institute (London, 1974).

4. Maryam Jameelah has reached a similar conclusion on Mawlana Mawdoodi. See her article in the *Islamic Quarterly, London: Journal of the Islamic Cultural Centre,* Vol 31, No 2, Second Quarter, 1987.

5. Hamid Algar, *op. cit.* p. 18.

6. For the Farsi text of the Imam's *fatwa*, see *Kayhan,* January 6, 1988. It was translated for me by Mr A Rafiee.

7. Moojan Momen, *An Introduction to Shi'i Islam,* Yale University Press, New Haven and London, 1985, pp 130-145.

8. 'Black boxing' is a method in scientific inquiry. It means that phenomena that cannot be explained in terms of a preferred theory or experiment are set aside in a 'black box' for later treatment. This allows theory and experimentation to proceed to the next stage. The 'black boxed' area is often resolved by subsequent progress in the discipline.

9. Kalim Siddiqui et al, *The Islamic Revolution: Achievements, Obstacles and Goals,* London: The Open Press, 1980, p. 14.

Glossary

'adl : justice, equality.

'alim : scholar learned in religious sciences, pl. 'ulama.

ayah : verse (in the Qur'an).

bida' : undesirable innovation in religion.

da'ii : one who invites unbelievers to believe in Islam.

Dar al-Islam : house of Islam or house of peace.

da'wah : invitation to Islam.

din : system that seeks to regulate all aspects of life according to revelation.

faqih : an expert of the science of Islamic laws *(fiqh).*

fatwah : a legal opinion given by a *faqih* or *'alim.*

fitnah : mischief, sedition or treason.

hadith : a saying of the Prophet.

hajj : pilgrimage to Makkah.

hikmah : method, wisdom.

haraam : forbidden.

hijab : headscarf used by Muslim women as part of their obligation to cover all parts of the body except face, hands and feet.

ibadah : formal or ritual prayer.

ijtihad : independent legal judgement on issues not settled in the Qur'an or by the precept, example or saying of the Prophet. One qualified to make such judgement is called *mujtahid.*

imam	:	Leader of the Muslim community or State; also one who leads Muslims in prayer or on a journey.
jahiliyyah	:	ignorant and immoral society, or state of Arab society before Islam.
jihad	:	total or any part of the struggle to defend or promote Islam or the Muslim community.
kafir	:	one who rejects belief in Allah.
majlis	:	Islamic Consultative Assembly (parliament) in Iran. Also a general term for any assembly called to decide issues affecting the community.
maraje'	:	pl. of *marja'*.
marja'	:	any 'Grand Ayatullah' who is considered worthy of emulation.
marjaiyyat	:	system of religious leadership of the *maraje'* among Shi'i Muslims.
malukiyyah	:	monarchy or dynastic rule.
muqallid	:	anyone who follows a *marja'*; pl. *muqallidin*.
muttaqi	:	committed to the path of Allah.
sahaba	:	companions of the Prophet.
sirah	:	Life of the Prophet.
sunnah	:	precepts and examples of the Prophet.
surah	:	chapter in the Qur'an.
ummah	:	the world community of all Muslims.
usulioon	:	those who follow the *usuli* school of thought among Shi'i Muslims.
Uthmaniyyah	:	Ottoman.

Index

133

F

Far East, the, 32
Fascism, 14, 76
Federation of Students' Islamic
    Societies (FOSIS), 22
Fidaiyan-e Islam, 53
FIS of Algeria, 52, 61
FLN of Algeria, 52, 61
France, 26, 35, 44, 48, 52, 61, 68
French Revolution, 68
Freudian psychology, 14
'fundamentalism', 18, 33

G

Ghazali, Imam, 103-104
Germany, 26, 68, 89
Global consensus, 38-46

H

Hambali school of thought, 12
Hamidullah, Dr Muhammad, 6
Hanafi school of thought, 12
Happiness, 74-75
Haramain, 5
Hijab, 44
Hijaz, 5, 22-23
Hilli, Allama (Jamaluddin Abu Mansur
    Hasan ibn Yusuf), 116
Hindus, 54, 57, 109
History, Divine purpose of, 49
    processes of, 107-130
    verdict of, 129
Hitler, 48
Hizbullah, 35, 48, 61, 75
Husain, Imam, 112, 119

I

Ijtihad, 4, 5, 15, 19, 72, 77, 101-102,
    113, 116, 121-122
Ikhwan al-Muslimoon, Al-, 19, 20, 23,
    32, 34, 36, 53, 85, 96 110, 121,
    124
'Islamicists', 21
Imam, 23
India, 26, 32, 54-59, 115

Information technology, 42
Intellectual revolution, 1, 9-16, 17, 18,
    21, 46, 47, 51, 77
International Federation of Students'
    Organisations (IFSO), 22
International Institute of Islamic
    Thought (IIIT), 22
Iqbal, Allama Dr Muhammad of Lahore,
    58
Iran, 19, 20, 42, 50
    CIA coup, 51, 79-91
Iraq, 20, 35, 49, 63, 115
Islam
    and America, 33
    and Europe, 17, 32
    and war, 89
    as knowledge, 3, 13-16
    correcting mechanism in, 44, 47,
    115-129
    deviation in, 108-129
    economic system, 96-97
    goals of, 3, 17
    historical record of, 7, 18, 49, 107
    Muslim women, 74
    obedience, 92-93, 95-96
    political system of, 5, 70-73
    power of, 24, 72, 77, 93-105, 120
    political regeneration, 15, 110,
    115-129
    worldview, 108
Islamabad, Islamic University of, 22
Islamic history, 28, 33, 49, 108-129
    building blocks of, 47, 50
Islamic parties
    and Islamic Revolution, 62-63,
    124
    democratic and moderate, 19, 45,
    50, 52, 85, 111
    failures of, 25, 36, 51, 61, 110
    in India, 54-59
    in nation-States, 34, 38, 112
Islamic fundamentalism 2, 18, 26
Islamic movement, global, 2, 5, 7, 18,
    20, 21, 27, 28, 35
    as Open University, 20, 25, 33,
    60, 105
    democratic approach, 45
    emergence of, 97-100
    goals of, 39, 40, 41, 44
    jihad in, 54-56, 58

North American Islamic Trust (NAIT), 22

North-West Frontier (of India), 55

O

Orientalism, 4
Othman dan Fodio, 98
Othman Ibn Affan, 40
Ottoman, 58 (see also Uthmaniyyah)
Owaisi, Latif and Zahida, 42

P

Pakistan, 18, 19, 21, 41, 48, 78, 115
   'Islamic State', 20, 59
Palestine, 17, 20, 26, 44, 49,
   Hamas, 61
   Islamic *jihad,* 61
Paris, 43
Partition of India, 57
Partial Islamic movements, 47-66
   in India, 54-59
Partial Islamic revolutions, 51
Pehlavi, 43, 114
Political consensus, 1, 41, 44, 49
Political systems, behaviour of, 68-78
Political thought, 1, 30-36, 41, 50
   in India, 54-59
Power, meaning of, 76-77
Public opinion, 95
Punjab, 55

Q

Qajar dynasty (of Iran), 50, 113
Qum, 114
Quraish of Makkah, 44, 70-72, 111, 126
Qutb, Sayyid, 21, 41, 73
Qutbzadeh, Sadeq, 82, 85

R

Rabita al-Alam al-Islami, 22
Rahman, Shaikh Omar Abdur, 53
Rajasthan, 55
Red Army, 48, 78
Reformation (of the Churches), 14
Renaissance, the, 14, 17, 35, 109

Riyadh, 22
Russia, 17, 68
Russian Empire, 49

S

Saddam Hussain, 64, 89
Safavid dynasty (of Iran), 5, 113
Safavid Shi'ism, 118
Sahaba (companions of the Prophet), 6,
   13, 71, 83
Salah al-Din Ayyubi, 120
Sanjabi, Karim, 82, 85
Satanic Verses, The, 27, 65
Saudi Arabia, 20, 21, 41, 64
   and Ikhwan, 21, 62-63
   and Jama'at-e Islami, 62-63
   court ulama, 114, 128
   da'wah, 111
   funding from, 22-23
   in Europe and North America, 21
   merchants, 22-24
   rulers of, 5, 19
   style 'Islamic States', 34, 40
Sayyid Ahmed Khan, Sir, 40, 56-58
Sayyid Ahmed Shahid, 54-56, 98
Sayyid Ismail Shahid, 54-56
Sepah (Revolutionary Guards in Iran),
   87
Serbia, 31
Shafa'i school of thought, 12
Shah Abdul Aziz, 54
Shah of Iran, 43
Shah Waliullah of Delhi, 54
Shamyl, Imam, 48
Shari'ati, Ali, 73
Shi'i
   conflict with Sunnis, 118
   diaspora (outside Iran), 19
   ijtihad in Shi'i tradition, 5,
   112-113
   mujtahids, 5
   theology, 19, 103, 110-129
Shirazi, Ayatullah Mirza Hasan, 50,
   102, 113
Shura, 93
Sikhs, 55-56
Sokoto *khilafah,* 98
Somalia, 48, 75